LIONS
TRIUMPHANT

Also by Sam Warburton

Refuse to be Denied

LIONS TRIUMPHANT

The Captain's Story

SAM WARBURTON

With Steve James

**SIMON &
SCHUSTER**

London · New York · Sydney · Toronto · New Delhi

A CBS COMPANY

First published in Great Britain by Simon & Schuster UK Ltd, 2013
A CBS COMPANY

1 3 5 7 9 10 8 6 4 2

Simon & Schuster UK Ltd
1st Floor
222 Gray's Inn Road
London WC1X 8HB

www.simonandschuster.co.uk

Simon & Schuster Australia, Sydney
Simon & Schuster India, New Delhi

Every reasonable effort has been made to contact copyright holders
of material reproduced in this book. If any have inadvertently been overlooked,
the publishers would be glad to hear from them and make good in future
editions any errors or omissions brought to their attention.

A CIP catalogue record for this book
is available from the British Library

ISBN: 978-1-47111-311-6
Ebook ISBN: 978-1-47111-314-7
Trade paperback ISBN: 978-1-47111-312-3

Typeset in the UK by M Rules
Printed and bound by CPI Group (UK) Ltd, Croydon, CR0 4YY

Contents

1

Getting the Call

Sunday, 21 April 2013.

It is a quiet Sunday afternoon in Rhiwbina, Cardiff, as I recover from playing for the Cardiff Blues the night before, in a match we had lost 24-6 to the Scarlets at Parc-y-Scarlets in Llanelli. I am at my parents' house with my fiancée Rachel. My mum, Carolyn, is on the phone to a friend. My own mobile phone is charging on the table in the kitchen. I hear it ring. Rather lethargically I go to it, thinking it is just a mate calling. I don't get there in time before it rings off.

I look at the screen. 'Missed Call Gats,' it says. That means that I have just missed a call from Warren Gatland, the head coach of the British and Irish Lions. Crikey! I haven't had a call from him for ages. This is no idle Sunday afternoon phone call.

All sorts of things start racing through my head. My heart starts pounding. 'This is it,' I think. This is about the captaincy of the Lions. It has to be. It is only nine days until the official squad announcement, after all. I knew that Warren was going to make a phone call to the player who was going to be captain of the Lions, because I had read that he had said that in the press. He'd commented that he had decided in his own mind on the person he was going to ask, but he was going to wait a while before doing so.

Ironically, around the time he had said this, I had met my agent Derwyn Jones for lunch at El Puerto's restaurant in Penarth Marina, Cardiff, and we had bumped into Warren, who was there meeting the Lions' strength and conditioning coach Adam Beard. Warren told me, after a brief handshake and hello, that he would be in touch soon, but he didn't say exactly what it was regarding.

Warren's comment had been at the back of my mind during the lunch when eventually Derwyn was the one to say: 'Do you think it's regarding the Lions captaincy?' It was what we had both been thinking for an hour, but neither of us had said anything. But the flip side of this was that there were obviously a few players in contention. So I also thought that he might want to call those guys who were close to being captain to tell them the disappointing news.

So, either way, this call had to be about the captaincy. Did I think it was going to be good news? Well, if you had asked me a month before the announcement to put some money on it, I would not have put that money on myself. I'd have put it on Brian O'Driscoll, if I'm honest. My parents had asked me that very question, and Brian had been the answer that I'd given them.

But then there had been a story in the press just a few days before that some of the bookmakers had stopped taking bets on me to be Lions captain. Apparently, Ladbrokes had had a lot of money placed on me, so they had suspended betting on my being captain and as a result slashed the odds of my starting the first Test as Lions captain in Brisbane on 22 June from 3-1 to 4-7.

Or so I was told anyway. I have to admit that I didn't understand that at first, because I don't bet. I truly didn't know whether suspending the betting was a good or a bad thing. But it was my dad who texted me to tell me about it. I said to him: 'What does that mean?' He replied it must mean: 'There's some inside information which has got out, or something like that.'

'Interesting,' I thought. Apparently, bookmakers have eyes and ears everywhere, so I started thinking there might be some truth in it. But at that stage I didn't know. I really didn't. It was then still 11 days away from the official team announcement.

After that Scarlets match I was put up for press duties, and inevitably I was asked about the fact that the bookmakers had closed betting on my becoming Lions captain. 'I can honestly say, on my mother's life, I have no inkling of anything,' I said. 'The players are often the last people to find out about these things, so I'll just keep my head down for the Blues. One minute it's [Paul] O'Connell, the next minute it's O'Driscoll, the next minute it's myself. It's difficult from a player's point of view. The decision is completely out of my hands. There's not much I can do, really, apart from wait for the announcement. Everybody is texting me, asking what's going on, which is really frustrating, because I genuinely don't know.'

The press asked me if I wanted to be captain, which was not as silly a question as it might sound, given that I have always been a rather reluctant captain. And remember, I hadn't been captain of Wales in the last two matches of the 2013 Six Nations that I started against Scotland and England.

'It's a no-brainer,' I said. 'It's the biggest honour for any player. It's mind-blowing when you think about it, to have that accolade. Everybody who has done it has been a legend and it's flattering to think you are in contention for it. I still don't see myself as one of those players, really. It's quite strange, especially at twenty-four. If somebody had told me when I was watching the last Lions tour [in 2009] that I could be in this situation as a potential candidate, I would have laughed. Obviously, it's an absolutely massive honour.

'Everybody is excited and looking forward to the squad announcement and what's going to happen. I'm still in the dark about that. Fingers crossed for all the boys. Players still aren't talking about it to each other. Honestly, they really don't want to talk about it. It's quite strange, it's quite funny. But hopefully there's a decent contingent from the Blues and Wales.

'It's in the back of your mind now, because it is getting very close to selection. You are desperate to go on tour. You are thinking about it quite a bit. I just have to keep my head down and keep my fingers crossed. I'll sit tight for the next few days and see what happens.'

That had been the night before. I probably wasn't going to have to sit tight or wait for a few days now. I probably wasn't going to have to wait for a few minutes. This phone call I was about to make could change my life. But what was Gats going to say to me?

I'd thought about the Lions so much already up to that point. I'd discussed it a lot with my family, and I don't mind admitting that I would get quite emotional when talking about it. I remember having dinner with Rachel a couple of years before and she suddenly asked me what was my greatest ambition in rugby. We don't usually talk about rugby when we're out, but on this occasion I became very emotional. I told her that my greatest ambition was to play for the Lions. It is the pinnacle. That's how much it meant to me. That's how desperate I was to get picked.

I had always wanted a framed Lions jersey up on my wall. That had long been an aspiration of mine. When I was 16, my parents had bought me a replica Lions jersey with a number seven on the back during the 2005 tour to New Zealand, and for quite a while afterwards I had worn it everywhere. It was my pride and joy. Then suddenly one day I made a decision. I'd had enough of that replica jersey. I took it off and vowed never to wear it again. It's still in my parents' house somewhere, but I said to myself: 'The next one I have to wear will be a proper one.' That's what's been pushing me ever since.

I had been thinking about the Lions announcement. I knew that it was going to take place on the morning of Tuesday 30 April, and it had already been said that only the captain would know in advance. Obviously, I wanted to be captain and so be told beforehand – or even told that I had missed out narrowly – but if none of that happened, I had thought about watching the announcement at the Cardiff Blues' training base at the Vale Resort, Hensol, near Cardiff.

I had pictured in my mind the TV being on in the canteen area, showing Sky Sports News with that announcement. All the squad would be there. I had thought about not looking too keen, because you wouldn't want to look arrogant. A few of the players might be watching you out of the corners of their eyes. I imagined it might be quite funny, because there was sure to be quite a bit of banter flying about, although you'd have to be careful about being too flippant if there were players in contention who did not make it.

Not that there had been much talk about the Lions all season at training. Nobody wanted to jinx themselves. I remember one day when winger Alex Cuthbert was waiting for a massage and he wrote his name 'Cuthie' on the massage sheet. Someone, just messing about, wrote next to it 'Lions 14'. He came back into the room, saw it and said: 'No chance,' straight away and scribbled it out. But now it seemed was the time to start talking about the Lions. I grabbed my phone and ran upstairs to my old bedroom, now used as a nursery by my parents for my little nephew, Harrison, when he visits. I shut the door and dialled the number.

Gats answered. We talked. And I have to say that he didn't get to the point very quickly! I was wishing he would. Firstly, he asked how my body was feeling after the Blues match, and

I replied that it had never felt better – which it hadn't. There were then some silences down the line during which I hoped he was going to give his reasons for calling me earlier.

And then, all of a sudden, he did give that reason. 'Do you want to be captain of the British and Irish Lions this summer?' he asked.

It was the most surreal question I've ever been asked. I'll repeat it. 'Do you want to be captain of the British and Irish Lions this summer?'

I started laughing at first. Maybe there was a little bit of swearing in there, too, because I couldn't believe what I'd just heard. Then very quickly I said: 'Yes, of course, I do. What an honour.'

Happy days! I ran down the stairs punching the air in delight. When I left my parents' house later that afternoon to walk down their driveway I was still doing the same. While it is a massive honour to captain your country, and it is always something I cherish and indeed something I hope to do in the future, this time my reaction was something more. Much, much more. This was pure joy.

When I was first made Wales captain in 2011, I was rather reluctant and nervy. But now I was just so happy and so sure in my own mind that it was a job I wanted to do and also one I knew I could do. I truly felt I was the right person to be captain of the Lions. There was not one shred of doubt. It was such a different feeling from when I was first asked to captain Wales, and it was also completely different from how I had felt just months earlier, when I had had problems with my belief in my own game and, as a result, the Wales captaincy. But we will come to that later.

Gats did not say a great deal more. There was not much more to say, but he did emphasise to me how important it was that this news was kept confidential until the day of the announcement. So did Greg Thomas, the Lions' head of media and communications, who phoned me later to stress that point as well. 'We can't have this coming out,' he said.

But I knew that I could tell my closest family. So I finished the call and rushed downstairs to tell Rachel first. There was no way I could have kept it from her. My mum was still on the phone. So I typed into my phone 'I'm captain of the Lions! C U later. Bye,' and showed it to her. Understandably, she lost all train of thought in her conversation and was totally lost for words. So she hurriedly told her friend she would call back and hung up, before giving me a huge hug.

My dad, Jez, was not at home. He was working at Whitchurch Fire Station in Cardiff (he has since retired). I just had to tell him, too. I made the phone call excitedly. I didn't beat about the bush. 'Warren has just phoned up and told me I'm going to be Lions captain,' I said.

He replied: 'Ah great, brilliant. OK ...'

He didn't seem exactly overjoyed. It threw me a bit. So I told him again. 'That's great, Sam,' he said. 'I'll give you a ring back in a few minutes.'

He eventually phoned me back about half an hour later. He was much more enthusiastic now. 'Sam, that's unbelievable news,' he began. So I started talking about it again, and then suddenly he went back to how he had been before. 'Yeah, OK. I'll talk to you later.'

I'd just told him the biggest piece of rugby news I could possibly give him, and done so twice, and he didn't seem that excited. I was baffled. But basically what had happened was that the first time I had phoned him, he was among his fireman colleagues at work. They love their rugby, and they were all desperate to find out if I was going to be Lions captain. My dad simply could not let on to them that I was phoning to tell him that I had just been appointed. Then, just when he thought he had found a quiet minute to speak to me later, someone else had walked into the room from which he was phoning. No matter. When he got home later he could say exactly what he wanted to say and show me how pleased he was with a big hug.

I didn't tell my brother, Ben, and sister, Holly, until the following Friday, before the official announcement took place on the next Tuesday. I felt bad about that, but I just couldn't risk it coming out. Ben was working as a physio at the Newport Gwent Dragons then (he has since moved to be with me at Cardiff Blues) and, while I know he would not have done so deliberately, he could easily have given it away accidentally by his reaction if one or two of the players had pressed him on it.

There was also my agent, Derwyn. He came to my house on the Wednesday for a catch-up and asked me if I knew anything about the captaincy. I told him that I knew nothing. But I knew that I had to tell him before the announcement, so I rang him on the Friday. He said he was delighted and then asked me one question: 'Did you know when I came to see you on Wednesday?'

I said I hadn't. I was lying. It was a couple of days after the announcement that he eventually told me that he knew I was captain when he came to see me on that Wednesday, because he had received a phone call from someone – let's just say that he is very resourceful. I apologised to Derwyn, but he just smiled and winked, as he'd known all along. He didn't put any pressure on me to tell him, but I still apologised. I found myself doing a lot of that around this time.

There was one other person I told before the announcement. That was Andy McCann, the Wales team psychologist with whom I have forged such a strong relationship. I asked him to come to my house on the Friday. He had no idea what for. 'I'm Lions captain,' I said immediately.

I wanted him to know early, because I knew he could help me with the role. He had helped me enormously when I had first been given the Wales captaincy in 2011. Then he had suggested that we make a leadership compass, a tool business leaders use a lot. We had come up with four qualities, one for each direction of the compass, from which I could draw strength. They were:

1. Professional attitude
2. Positive attitude
3. Develop personal relationships with the players
4. Most importantly my own performance, and leading by example.

Getting the Call

I had saved this compass on my iPhone so that I could refer to it regularly. And, at Andy's instigation, we had also put together a book called *Warby's Winning Ways*, which I have used ever since as both inspiration and motivation. It included all sorts of things from that leadership compass, to positive press clippings and photographs of me playing well, along with photos of my family (including one of my twin brother Ben on his own, because I have always played every game for him after he was injured and had to give up the game), Rachel and even my dogs, to a list of my heroes like boxer Lennox Lewis, Andy himself and my former schoolteacher Gwyn Morris. We had even put in there the sponsorship deals I'd achieved, because Andy felt that it was important that I recognised my rewards.

So we now went over all of this again, and we updated the 'WWW' book for the Lions. And one of the quotes in there I actually used later on the tour in a press conference when I was asked about the goal for the tour before the Queensland Reds game. I said it was to win every game. 'It takes no more energy to have a bigger goal than a smaller goal,' I said. I like that quote. It suits me well because I am so optimistic and ambitious. Andy laughed when I told him that I had used it in a press conference, but I'm not sure it was used by any of the journalists there.

On that Friday together, Andy and I also came up with a specific plan to tackle the Lions captaincy. It wasn't that we didn't think I could cope with it; it was just that, between us, we wanted to make sure that I was fully prepared for it. I wanted to be as meticulous in preparing myself for it as I would be with my training, nutrition and sleep. Andy decided to call it the 'Captain's Corner', and it was a grid to which I could refer throughout the tour if I came across any captaincy problems.

We agreed upon six scenarios that I could possibly face and what I might do about them. So one might be that I felt there were too many press demands on me at a certain time, or that I fancied some time on my own. Another might involve some of the players coming up to me and saying that they were tired. So I had to work out when that might happen, and whom I would talk to in order to deal with it.

Other situations we considered were more specific, for example what would I do if the tight-five forwards were tired and sore, and we had a big scrummaging session to come and we had not covered scrummaging that week. There is always a fine balance between having to do scrummaging but not wanting to tire out the tight-five forwards, who do go through a lot of wear and tear during the week. So if Paul O'Connell, as scrum leader, came up to me and said these things, then we decided that I would go to the tight-head props Adam Jones and Dan Cole as reference points, as well as forwards coach Graham Rowntree and Adam Beard, who would have all the GPS data and could say whether we had overworked or underworked during a week.

I wrote all these six scenarios down, and alongside them I added which coaches or players I might speak to, so that if any of the scenarios did occur then I would be able to deal with them swiftly and easily. But the truth is that hardly any of them did occur, and I didn't have to refer to the 'Captain's Corner' half as much as I thought I would have to.

Certainly that scrummaging instance didn't occur. That's because we were managed brilliantly. As always, Warren Gatland was adamant that the training sessions should be short and sharp. If he said that the session was going to last only 41 minutes, he made sure it lasted 41 minutes. That's how he operates.

There were a couple of instances early in the tour where, say, Graham Rowntree was taking unit sessions in the morning, and Gats would give him 30 minutes to do so. And occasionally they would last nearly 45 minutes. So at the next squad meeting, Gats would give Wig, as everyone knows Graham Rowntree, some banter about his sessions running over, and Wig would give plenty of banter back. But Gats was making a subtle point and it worked, because for the rest of the tour, all the sessions were spot on.

However, while I was able to plan for the captaincy with Andy, I still couldn't tell anyone else about it, and that was so difficult. There were several awkward situations I had to deal with, and so many people I would have loved to have told, but I couldn't. It was so tough to keep it quiet for nine or ten days. Even other family members were asking me about it and I had to lie to them. I lied to many good friends, as well. Everyone was asking if I had heard anything, and I was just saying that I hadn't. When the news finally came out, I got a lot of sarcastic texts from mates. I apologise to all those that I misled, but I hope they can all understand why now.

If it is any consolation to them, it was agony, because I just had to keep this massive secret. My team-mates at the Cardiff Blues were trying to trick me into revealing something. They kept asking me if I was going to be at training on the Monday before the announcement, knowing full well that the captain would probably have to go up to London that day. And Jamie Roberts even went a bit further. He said that he had an important charity function on that Monday night, and asked me if I could go along with him as a special guest. I had to tell him I was busy, but he was looking at me with a strange smile, waiting for a reaction. I think he knew, but I couldn't tell him.

I did actually go to Blues training on that Monday, but then I was picked up straight afterwards by Jon Davis, the Six Nations operations director and British Lions secretary, who lives not far from me in Rhiwbina. He took me up to the outskirts of London to the Hilton Hotel in Syon Park, where the announcement was to be made the next day, and where I stayed that night.

I was picked up in a Land Rover, and most of the Blues boys knew that the Lions were sponsored by them, so when they saw me being driven off in one of those vehicles, they texted me to ask what was going on. I had to keep trying to be as secretive as I could, though. When I got to the hotel, we had to go to the back entrance and I had to walk through the underground of the hotel to a private lift taking me up to my room. I just couldn't afford to be seen because we knew, for instance, that the BBC Wales crew were staying in that hotel that night in readiness for the announcement the next day.

I had a meal that night with all the coaches, management and committee, but it was in a private room at the hotel. Before that I had walked into the room just as the coaches were finishing picking the squad. That's what they told me anyway, and I do know that there was some last-minute agonising.

It was the first time I had seen Warren since his phone call, so it was good to see him and the other coaches. Warren then asked me: 'Do you want to have a look at the squad?'

I was like a kid at Christmas. I was going to get a sneak pre-view of the squad, although there was a part of me that was worried whether I would be able to resist telling my mates in the Wales squad. Anyway before I did have a look at it, Warren said to me: 'If you could pick one wild card, who would it be?'

I replied: 'Well, I think you know who I would want to pick.'

'Who?' he asked, even though I think he knew full well who I was on about.

'The Chopper,' I said.

'Who? Dan?' he asked. We were talking about Dan Lydiate, who gets his name because he is renowned for his famous chop tackles. I suddenly realised that this was going to be really awkward if he had not been picked.

'Why would you pick him?' questioned Warren.

'Because I think that he can do things other players can't,' I replied.

Warren said no more and showed me the piece of paper. My eyes went straight to the back row where there were the names of Sam Warburton, Dan Lydiate, Justin Tipuric and Toby Faletau. Four Welsh boys in the back row, including my great mate Dan! I was so happy. In all there were 15 Welshmen. As well as the four of us, there was also Leigh Halfpenny, George North, Alex Cuthbert, Jamie Roberts, Jonathan Davies, Mike Phillips, Gethin Jenkins, Richard Hibbard, Adam Jones, Alun-Wyn Jones and Ian Evans.

In the selected squad, there were also ten English players: Manu Tuilagi, Owen Farrell, Ben Youngs, Tom Youngs, Mako Vunipola, Matt Stevens, Dan Cole, Geoff Parling, Dylan Hartley (though he was replaced before the tour began by Ireland's Rory Best after he was sent off in the Aviva Premiership final) and Tom Croft; nine Irishmen: Brian O'Driscoll, Tommy Bowe, Rob Kearney, Jonathan Sexton, Conor Murray, Cian Healy, Paul O'Connell, Sean O'Brien and Jamie Heaslip; and three Scots: Stuart Hogg, Sean Maitland and Richie Gray.

I could so easily have sneaked off and texted Dan to tell him. I knew that he was really fretting over the announcement, and that he thought he was going to be off to Japan with Wales. If he had played in the Six Nations, it would have been different – he would have been one of the first names on the teamsheet after his performances in the 2012 tournament – but, because of the terrible ankle injury that he had suffered at the start of the season, he had been able to play only a few games for the Newport Gwent Dragons before the squad was announced.

Happily, he had done enough, and I so wanted to give him the good news. I knew I couldn't, though. He had to find out through the same channels as everyone else. But I did tell Rachel that he was in. She knew how pleased he would be, and how pleased I was for him.

Even on that Tuesday morning, I still had to keep a low profile. I had to have room service for breakfast and could not go out of my room until just before 11am. If any of the media had seen me, they would have known immediately that I was captain. I heard there were rumours that someone had seen Paul O'Connell there, and so the story spread that he had got the job. There were so many media people present that day, there was no way I could move about the place. It was a huge event.

The subterfuge continued when I had to hide downstairs in the kitchens while everyone moved into a ballroom decked out in red, with Lions logos and those of all of the corporate partners for the tour around the room. By now I was so nervous. I met the guys doing the Lions DVD for the first time, and it made me think immediately of all the other DVDs about the Lions and how good they were. Now I was going to be in one of them.

I was waiting outside the ballroom and it was a very weird sensation, because I knew that at that very moment all the players in England, Wales, Scotland and Ireland would be crowding around TVs to see the squad. It was awesome to hear the names read out and to imagine how they might have been reacting.

The MC for the event was Sky Sports' Alex Payne, and after some preliminaries and the announcement of the rest of the squad, Warren took to the podium and said: 'I am pleased to announce that the captain of the 2013 British and Irish Lions is Sam Warburton.'

The lights were dimmed and my fact file appeared up on the big screen as I entered the room dressed in a Lions shirt. I walked the length of the room up to the big stage. It was an unbelievable feeling to do that. This was it: I really was Lions captain now. Apparently, I was only the fifth Welshman to be selected as Lions tour captain, and the first since Phil Bennett in 1977, and, at 24, I was also the youngest Lions captain in nearly 60 years.

I sat between Warren and the tour team manager Andy Irvine on one side of the stage, while the four other coaches – Graham Rowntree, Andy Farrell, Rob Howley and Neil Jenkins – sat on the other side. Eventually, I was interviewed on stage by Alex and I told him the story of receiving the call from Warren nine days previously. 'It's unbelievable – an accolade that very few people are able to achieve. To have the opportunity to do this is an unbelievable honour,' I added.

'It's going to be new for me. I am going to learn along the way. I can't sit here and say I know what will happen, because I don't. There is a good Welsh contingent of leaders that I know I can rely on, and there are leaders from other countries whose help I am sure I will need along the way. It's an experience that I just can't wait to get underway now. I'm very much looking forward to the squad meeting up. I'm always the ultimate optimist. I will go out there with the intention to win every match. That will be the great challenge for the players, as no other Lions team has done that.'

There followed a whole host of interviews with various media outlets: TV, radio and written press, with the latter divided up into Sunday and daily papers. It was a long day, but it was still enjoyable. If you can't be happy about being Lions captain, when can you be?

I was driven back to Cardiff that evening, and picked up my car; it was about 5.20pm and I was not far from home when I spoke to Rachel. She asked where I was. I told her, and she suddenly started acting a little strangely. 'Sam, go and get some milk, will you please?' she said.

'I bought six pints before I went,' I replied. 'We don't need any milk.'

'Sam, just go and get some milk please,' she said.

'Rach, I'm still in my Lions kit. The team has only been announced today, and if I go into Spar with that on, everyone will think I'm a big head.'

I didn't have a clue what was going on, so I thought I would pop into my parents' house on the way home. I got there and they were all dressed up ready to go out.

'Where are you going?' I asked.

They replied that they were going to the Deri Inn in Rhiwbina near their house for a few drinks. 'I'll come with you,' I said.

'No, no, you go home and see Rachel when she gets back from work,' they said. 'You can come and see us later.'

21

'Oh, and Rachel just phoned me and said that you have to go and get some milk,' said my mum.

'Why do I have to go and get some milk?' I was asking myself. Something odd was going on, but I had no idea what it was. So I went to the Spar, rushed in, got some milk, and rushed out again.

I went home, and by this time Rachel was there. She came to the door and, as she did so, she shut the lounge door. She was acting very weirdly, because usually when I have been away for a bit I will often come through the door and say something overly romantic just for a bit of fun, and she will enjoy that. But when I did that now, I got hardly any reaction back from her. All she said was: 'There is a surprise present for you in the lounge.' So I opened the door, and there were all my family and Rachel's family waiting to give me a surprise party to celebrate being named Lions captain. All that fuss about the milk had been Rachel trying to buy some time to make sure she was home from work before I was. It was a really nice gesture from all of them, and I really appreciated it. It was a lovely evening.

I still couldn't believe it all, to be honest. There were banners up in my house saying congratulations on being Lions captain, but still it wouldn't sink in. At one stage I glanced at the TV and saw the writing at the bottom of the screen saying 'Sam Warburton British and Irish Lions captain'. I paused the picture, grabbed my phone and took a photo of it. It was surreal.

I thought back to being in my hotel room that morning and

going to the bathroom, and as I did so, I looked at the mirror, and there was the Lions badge on my polo shirt. It was only a polo shirt, but I remember thinking 'Wow! I'm going to be a Lion. And captain, too.'

As I had said in one of the interviews that day about being a Lion: 'From a young kid, it's always something that I've wanted to do. The captaincy has never been in my mind, which is why it's such a shock and I'm so delighted. First things first is the performance, though. That's the most important thing you have to prioritise as captain. The one reservation I've always had about captaincy is making sure you don't become complacent. If you are captain, then you don't want to assume that you are always going to be picked. I don't like that. I like it when you go to the team announcements and you are on the edge, you don't know whether you are picked or not.'

There were some very complimentary words for me from Warren sitting alongside me, who also made sure that I wasn't lulled into any complacency. 'Sam is a quiet man who also leads from the front. I think he will do a brilliant job,' he said. 'Paul [O'Connell] and Brian [O'Driscoll] were considered [for the captaincy], but if I was picking a Test side tomorrow Sam would be in that side, be it at six or seven. A number of other players will be fighting for positions. I think a lot has been made of this year, but one of the things I admire about Sam is that it is not about him, it is about putting the team first. But he is under no illusions – his performances have to be good enough.'

There had also been some interesting comments from Warren

about my rapport with referees and how that influenced his selection. 'I saw something happen in the Wales v England game when [referee] Steve Walsh penalised Sam,' he said. 'And he allowed him to go to him three times on one occasion to question a decision and get some clarification. Walsh does not allow that from anybody, and it was a big signal to me that either referees have been talking or they all respect him, because there are only two or three players in the world who would have been allowed to do that. It really stuck in my mind. His ability to communicate and strike a rapport with referees could potentially have a positive influence on the game.

'I am not concerned about the referees we have for the three Tests [Chris Pollock, Craig Joubert and Romain Poite] and I think the portents are good. Wales have had Craig Joubert on a number of occasions and he is fair. He has a really good relationship with Sam and, having spoken to him, I know he has a really good relationship with Sam, rating him as one of the best opensides in the world. When a referee tells you that he enjoys his leadership, has a rapport with him, likes refereeing Sam and respects him as a player, it was quite an easy decision to make to appoint him as captain.'

What sort of Lions captain was I going to be? That was a question being asked a lot. For a start, I was pretty sure that I was going to be one of the quietest captains the Lions had ever had. But I knew that I was the type of captain Warren wanted. I think it has been well documented that I was shocked when he first asked me to be captain of Wales in 2011. And that was because I did not consider myself a leader in any way. I thought a captain was the man who stood up and made a lot of noise. But I was wrong. There is much more to captaincy than that.

I remember Warren showing me some videos of my behaviour on the pitch, the way I was communicating, the way I'd go in for a big hit when the lads' chins were down, and he said: 'That's leadership.' It was those traits he wanted more than being able to give a good speech in the dressing room. Leading by example is the term everyone uses. That's what I try to do.

The other aspect of captaincy that initially worried me was that I don't like being singled out. I'm at my best when I'm backed into a corner. I need to feel those butterflies in my stomach that come if you think you're not going to be picked. As captain I have never wanted to be closer to the coaches than the other players. I think everyone should have the same relationship. And that is certainly the case with Warren and me.

So as a captain I'm not a motivator, screaming and shouting at people. I'm not one for the up-and-at-'em speeches before a match. In fact, I'll usually speak for no more than 30 seconds before we go out on to the field as a team. I don't even usually think about what I'll say until I'm on the bus on the way to the game. When I do eventually speak, a lot of those 30 seconds will be taken up by tactical talk, making sure players know what their roles are in the first five minutes. Make a mistake in that time and it can have massive consequences. I always leave the head banging to the front five. That's what they are good at. They love that sort of thing.

Some might argue that I'm probably too laid back for my own good in that regard. I don't study leadership, and I don't go looking for too much guidance (although, of course, I will gladly accept help and support), I just try to act naturally. My view is that people can over-complicate things, whether in leadership, rugby or anything else.

One of the best pieces of advice I had when talking about the captaincy was 'just be yourself'. It sounds very simple, but in reality it is not always that simple. A lot of people try to be something or someone just for the sake of others. That has never been my way of doing things. I'm not one to talk about families, fans or countries when speaking to my team. There are no Churchillian speeches. If I tried that, people would know it's not me. Yes, of course, I get pumped up before a game, but it's just that it doesn't come out in what I say.

Warren knew all this when appointing me as captain. He knew what he was getting in me as a captain. And I knew I would not let him down. The decision had been made. I was overjoyed. It was time to get started. It was no time to be worrying what people thought of the decision to make me captain. I was not going to watch or read anything on that matter.

Well, I wasn't, until I made a bad mistake in watching a Sky Sports Rugby Club programme on which they were discussing my appointment. They started talking about it and I thought to myself 'I should turn over now', but instead I kept watching. The consensus seemed to be that either Paul O'Connell or Brian O'Driscoll should have been made captain. I suppose I could understand that. I think the Welsh people knew what I could do, because they had seen more of me, but those from other countries would have wanted someone from their country to be captain. But still I got a little angry. 'I can't wait to prove these people wrong,' I thought.

It was just under two weeks later that we assembled as a squad for the first time, meeting at Syon House as we were kitted out for the tour and we sorted out all our administrative stuff like visas, as well as having the official tour photo taken. Some of the boys said it was like a first day at school, and it certainly was. There was a lot of excitement about what lay ahead.

And as for the amount of kit given to us by Adidas, well, it was monumental. Not that anyone was complaining! There were personalised boots, and the level of detail in general was remarkable – we were even measured up for recovery skins to wear on all of our various flights throughout the tour. This was done by a laser instrument that measured the exact size of our calves and ankles.

We arrived there in dribs and drabs, but all the Welsh boys had got there first, having come up on a bus from Cardiff. I was amazed at the tension among us, especially as we were used to one another's company – it was another moment that showed why the Lions are different. I remember George North saying: 'I can't believe how nervous I am!' Some of them were urging me to go in first as we arrived.

I thought that I knew most of the squad already, but then when I got there, I realised that I didn't really. I'd met Paul O'Connell at a Six Nations launch, and I'd shared a table with Jamie Heaslip after a Six Nations match, I'd had a chat with

Sean O'Brien after another Six Nations match, and I'd met Manu Tuilagi at a sponsor's function – and got on with him straight away – but other than that it was a question of getting to know new team-mates.

It was quite quiet, really. It's always interesting to see how people react to that new environment, treading carefully at first as they size up each other's personalities. You find that it is not until the second or third week of a tour that everyone is comfortable with everyone else's personalities.

I remember walking to have the team photo alongside Geoff Parling, and I asked him what some of the boys' nicknames were. That created some fun through the tour. He told me that Tom Croft was called 'Yog', but the one I found most amusing was that Owen Farrell is called 'Foxy Bingo' after the fox on the TV advert. I didn't know Owen at all at this stage, but as most of the Welsh boys usually add 'boy' after calling someone's name, when I walked past Owen I said casually: 'Foxy Bingo boy.'

He was taken aback. 'How did you know about that?' he asked, before bursting out laughing.

Cian Healy is known as 'Church' and for quite a while I was careful not to swear around him because I genuinely thought he was very religious. Eventually, I asked him and he told me the story behind it. He said himself that everyone expects it to be a great story, but it's actually pretty rubbish. I think I'm right in saying that it is not because he is particularly religious and we'll leave it at that!

I didn't know what to call Ben Youngs. We named his

brother Tom 'Younger', but I was having to make do with just 'Ben' or 'Youngy' for the scrum-half, so I asked him what I should do. He said that he was known as 'Lenny'. So that's what I started trying to do but, because I had been calling him 'Ben', I started getting a little tongue-twisted – and I know George North had this same problem, too – so that I ended up saying 'Blenny'. That became mine and George's special nickname for him!

There were only two players unavailable for that get-together: Gethin Jenkins, because of commitments with his French side Toulon, and Brian O'Driscoll, who was advised not to fly over to London from Dublin, after he had hurt his back playing for Leinster against Glasgow in the RaboDirect Pro12 league. The injury forced him out of Leinster's Amlin Challenge Cup final win over Stade Francais.

Warren asked if I would speak to the squad. I won't say that I relished doing that, but I simply had to. The players would have been expecting something from me. The first thing I said was that any help from the experienced leaders within the group would be much appreciated, but I also emphasised the role the younger players could play, too. 'Just because it's your first tour, it doesn't mean you can't have a say, and the young players have so much energy it's important for them to be heard, as this can drive a team along.'

I also mentioned about the mentality of winning. 'If anybody asks you about whether we can win, just tell them that you expect to do so. It's not about hoping to do so, it's about expecting it, and that is a mindset that has to be there

throughout the tour party, from the players through to management and back-room staff. It's an attitude that will drive us
forwards.'

Basically, my speech was about the honour and privilege of
being a Lion. But I also thought that I would use a true story
about something that had happened to me only just before this.

About a week before we gathered for the first time, Leigh
Halfpenny and I had made a hospital visit in Cardiff. The wife
of our director of rugby, Phil Davies, had asked us to go to
see a young boy who was dying of cancer. It was so moving.
He had lost both his legs and he could barely speak, but he
loved watching rugby. And he was so upbeat talking about it.
We signed all his shirts and scarves for him, and you could see
that we had made his day. But as we left the hospital, Leigh
and I looked at each other. It was a look that said: 'We are both
so lucky.' It was an extremely emotional and heartbreaking
moment for both of us. Tragically, we discovered that soon
afterwards the young boy died.

I told this story to the Lions players and concluded:
'Imagine the joy we gave to that boy. If only I could have had
the power to say to him: "You will be OK. You'll play for the
Lions one day." That is what we have got. We are doing something that so many people would love to do. Wherever you
are, whether it is thinking about doing extra weights or any
extra training, please bear that in mind.'

I hoped that was a strong message. 'None of us should ever
forget how lucky we are,' I added. ' I don't think we will.'

And I don't think we did.

2

Man Down

Confession time. I turned down the Wales captaincy for the final match of the Six Nations campaign against England in Cardiff. That's the first time that I have admitted that publicly. Coach Rob Howley knew that I was probably going to turn it down, because I had already told him before the previous match against Scotland that I was not keen to be captain, even though he had already just told me that Ryan Jones would be captain for that match. Also, before the Six Nations had even begun, I was actually thinking of phoning Rob to tell him that I didn't want to be captain.

Why? There were many reasons. As I've already mentioned, I was always a rather reluctant captain in the first place, but the problem during the early part of the Six Nations was that, with injuries not helping either, I was beginning to lose my confidence as a player. And the truth is that I was not sure that I deserved to be captain. I was not even sure I deserved to be in the side. So many people in Wales were saying that the Ospreys' in-form Justin Tipuric should be at openside flanker that I think I started to believe them. I had let the press get to me. I usually have so much self-belief, but all the comments saying that I shouldn't be playing for Wales got to me.

Obviously I wasn't playing as well as I had at the World Cup in 2011, but in the last two matches of the autumn series against New Zealand and Australia, I thought I had played well. I also had the highest number of turnovers in the RaboDirect Pro12. But people weren't seeing that and the upshot was that all the pervading negativity was engulfing me, and I wasn't taking the field with as much confidence as I should have been.

I don't read the press much, but even so you are indirectly affected by it. My mum and dad were certainly aware of what was being written and said. They were constantly worried about the press reaction after any game. They weren't worried about how good a game I'd had, instead their instant thoughts were about what other people would say about it. That is not right, but that is how they were feeling before the England match.

It was then that Rob came to me and asked if I would be captain for the deciding game, because Ryan, who had stood in as captain against France, Italy and Scotland after I had been captain against Ireland, was injured. I told him that I did not want to do it, because I just wanted to concentrate on my own game. I honestly felt that that was best for everyone. It was certainly best for the team.

I had thought that Rob might ask me to take over again, even though I had already told him that I didn't want to do it. He might have thought that the reason I didn't want to take it on was out of respect for Ryan, and that now he was injured my opinion might have changed. But that wasn't part of my thinking at all. I had been so happy with my preparation for the Scotland match, where I had just been able to sit quietly and focus on my own game, that I did not want to change that.

I remember sitting there thinking when Rob offered it to me: 'I could do this now. I could have on my CV two Six Nations championships as well as a World Cup semi-final, all as captain.' But I concluded: 'I don't want to do it just for that reason. It would be wrong.' I felt I needed to focus on my own performance. I was so low on confidence that I thought the captaincy might hinder that, and therefore having the distraction would harm the team's performance. After all, if I could produce another personal performance like I had at Murrayfield, where I was man of the match and we won, then I knew that it would be good for the team.

So what changed so much that I could take on the Lions captaincy with such confidence and determination? The simple answer is the form I showed in those last two games of the Six Nations against Scotland and England. I rediscovered my confidence there and with it my entire outlook on rugby improved. You can't just feel on top of your game throughout your whole career. I'd been in a rut, but those games against Scotland and England had dragged me out of it.

And I didn't feel so bad when I read an article that someone pointed me towards, where Brian O'Driscoll said he once consulted a sports psychologist, Enda McNulty, during the

2007-08 season because he was so low on confidence. If a true great of the game like Brian can get so low, then we all can.

The truth of it was I'd had a difficult tournament in the Six Nations; there is no denying that. The first game at home against Ireland went really badly for us, especially in a first half in which we found ourselves 23-3 down after tries from Simon Zebo and Cian Healy, with Jonathan Sexton kicking 13 points. That all got even worse just after half time when Brian scored and, with the conversion, it was 30-3. What's more, we had already lost seven games on the trot (three to Australia in the previous summer, then to Argentina, Samoa, New Zealand and Australia again in the autumn internationals).

With the four Welsh regions not doing particularly well at the time, it was all doom and gloom in Welsh rugby, a feeling that sadly enveloped me at one stage. Everybody was talking about how we had fallen from grace after reaching the semi-finals of the 2011 Rugby World Cup and then winning the Grand Slam in 2012. But I knew that we had the players, especially if everyone could get themselves fit. And looking back now, I'm pretty happy that after this Ireland defeat, I wrote these words in my *Daily Telegraph* column:

'There is a lot of talk about a crisis in Welsh rugby, but the team has not been looking at it like that at all. Looking from a Six Nations point of view, even though we have lost the first game and the Grand Slam has gone, what people have got to remember is that not many championships are won through Grand Slams. Most teams will lose a game somewhere. The championship is still up for grabs.'

That's not to say that the Ireland match wasn't disappointing. We were just generally inaccurate. We simply weren't at the races in the first half: we hadn't been competing on the ball enough, and we hadn't slowed Ireland's ball down at all. In contrast, Ireland were doing a very good job of slowing our ball down. They were making good use of their famous choke tackle tactic, and there were two turnovers from it in the first half. The rest of the time they were just using it to slow down our ball. And they were doing it very well.

In fairness, we rallied really well. We scored three tries through Alex Cuthbert, Leigh Halfpenny and Craig Mitchell, and we put Ireland under so much pressure that both Conor Murray and Rory Best were given yellow cards, but we still fell short at 30-22. Afterwards, as there seemed to be for much of the season, there already seemed to be a lot of talk about my form and even, at this very early stage, about how it might affect selection for the Lions. As I have already stated, I can honestly say that the 'L' word was not being mentioned among our squad then.

What put the debate into context was that Justin Tipuric was having a really good season, and when he came on at seven as a replacement (with me moving to six) in this match he made an obvious difference to our attacking play. It began a huge debate that ran and ran. All I can say is that I actually enjoyed playing alongside him. We often found ourselves at the same ruck in that Ireland match and that worked quite well in clearing the ball out in that second half. In fact, I thought that I was going to be starting that match at six, because that was where I had trained for much of the time in preparation, but then when the team announcement came, I was at seven and Aaron Shingler was at six.

After the match I wrote in my *Daily Telegraph* column: 'I am reasonably happy with my form at this time. I am always looking to improve, but I spoke to the coaches and team analysts and I got their approval, which is what always counts to me most. If I was falling off tackles and getting smashed around, it might be different, but I am not.

'I am always honest in talking about my performance. In fact one of our analysts, Rhys Long, came up to me after the game and asked what I would have given myself out of ten for my performance. I said six. He said he thought I was being harsh on myself. But I was annoyed with some things I did, like dropping a line-out, which I don't normally do, and getting penalised for obstruction once, even if I think that was a harsh decision.

'I didn't get a turnover, which is always frustrating. I usually target three or four a game. I looked back at the video and I got in over the ball seven or eight times, but the Irish double-teamed and cleaned me out every single time. I was in position over the ball, but couldn't quite manage to grab it. But I would have been a lot more worried if I hadn't been getting in those positions in the first place.

'In attack, I had about nine carries, with which I was pleased and I made the most tackles among our team. As captain I admit now that I made the wrong decision by opting for a kick to the corner on 68 minutes, when Murray was sin-binned, and the score was 30-15. We should have taken the three points. That was my decision and nobody else's, and I got it wrong. I normally always take the three points when they are on offer. My thought process is that if we are more than two scores behind with about ten minutes to go, then I go for the corner. This instance made me change that thinking. We would have had ten minutes to score two tries, which is doable.'

I was trying to remain positive, which, of course, you must do, but I look back now and realise that I wasn't good enough in that Ireland match. The fact that I did not get a turnover was just not acceptable. That is my job.

Unfortunately, I also got what is called a 'compression stinger' in my left shoulder, while cleaning out Sean O'Brien from a ruck. I get them in the other side of my body from which I make a tackle, as my head side-flexes and the discs in my neck compress. I did not think it was going to be too serious, and that I would be fit for the match in France the following week. When I missed training on the Tuesday, it seemed more like a precaution than anything else.

So I was fully expecting to travel to Paris after the team announcement on the Thursday. My fiancée Rachel had even gone to stay with her parents for the weekend in anticipation of my being away. But then on the Thursday morning at 9am, I was assessed by the medical staff and it was decided that I was not fit enough to play. They were doing tests that did not even involve contact work, and I was still in a lot of pain doing those. It was definitely the right decision.

There really is something unlucky about the French for me. Three times I have played against them and I have not made it into the second half in any of those games. First there was the Six Nations match at Stade de France in 2011 when I injured my knee ligaments early in the match, then there was the much-talked-about red card in the World Cup semi-final later in the year, and then in 2012 in the Grand Slam-clincher in Cardiff I was forced off at half time with a nerve problem in my right shoulder.

And now there was this one, when I did not even get on the team bus. I had been told privately that I was going to be wearing number six, as well, with Justin at seven. As it was, Ryan Jones, who had been injured for the Ireland game, came in, and as captain too for a record 30th time. What a match he had. It was a game that, against the odds, Wales won 16-6, and Ryan was quite superb. I knew he would be. I just knew that he would do a great job as captain and flanker. He is so experienced and smart on a rugby field, and he was so desperate to end our long run of defeats. I texted him straight afterwards to congratulate him, and to say well done to all the lads.

It was such a good win. In many ways, it was the perfect match to get our campaign back on track. The boys simply didn't have anything to lose. People might have been surprised, but the squad was still very confident, despite the run of losses. We had been preparing for a backlash. France had lost to Italy in Rome the week before and we knew that they would be a very different proposition at home against us.

We always said before the World Cup that we would play

without any fear. Perhaps that wasn't the way we approached that first half against Ireland. Maybe we were a little bit too conservative. In Paris, the boys just went out and expressed themselves from the off. I certainly got very excited watching it at home. Rachel and I were dressed, ready to go straight after the game for a meal in Newbridge-on-Usk, where the Celtic Manor resort have a restaurant off-site. I needn't have bothered as I had to change my shirt before we could go anywhere, because I had been sweating so much at the tension of the game.

I felt like I was a 15-year-old again watching Wales, or a bit like I am all the time these days when watching Spurs play football. I was going mad. One minute I'd be punching the air, and then the next I'd have my head in my hands thinking 'It's so hard to keep France out for the last ten minutes! You just never know!'

We were 13-6 up and I was worried that seven points weren't going to be enough, so when we got a penalty with six minutes left I shouted: "That's it! Leigh will bang it over!' I was confident we would win then. And, of course, he did send the kick over, and then he was named man of the match afterwards. That was to become a recurring theme in the months ahead. What a player he is.

Three minutes earlier, George North had scored the crucial try. And I was delighted for him. Like a few of us, he had been under a bit of pressure about his form, but he is a world-class player and he showed that there and has gone on to do so again and again since. I also texted him to say congratulations – 'world-class finish,' I said – and promised him a hug on the Monday morning. And, of course, that was what he had had from his dad after scoring, for this was the well-publicised incident when his dad rushed on to the field in Paris to celebrate his son's try. I knew it was George's dad straight away. I recognised his moustache. I'd met him quite a few times in the family room at the Millennium Stadium, and he has become good mates with my dad, so I said to Rachel "I'm sure that was George's dad!"

We paused the TV coverage on that moment and, sure enough, it was him! I spoke to George on the Monday – after giving him that hug, of course! – and he said that his dad had had a feeling that George was going to do something in that corner of the ground where he was sitting. He certainly did that.

Rachel and I stayed in Newbridge-on-Usk that night, just because I had to get away from it. Despite the excitement of the match and the joy for my colleagues, I was what you might call a 'man down' at this stage. I really was at a low point. It was at this moment that I started thinking I was not the best seven in Wales. My identity statement when I began seeing Andy McCann was 'I am a world-class seven', but, as I have developed as a player, it has turned into 'I am the world's best seven'.

I hope that doesn't sound big-headed. It's just that I have to take to the field with that mindset. It's what I have tried to do since I was a young boy, always believing that I am better than my opposite number. That identity statement is what I will say to myself before a game, but there were times during the

2012-13 season when I did not want to say it before a game simply because I did not believe it myself.

I had lost so much self-belief. Derwyn Jones, my agent, gave me a bit of a bollocking about that when I eventually told him what I had been going through. We'd had a similar conversation during the autumn internationals prior to the All Blacks game, so he knew that things weren't quite right with me again this time.

Derwyn is more than an agent to me. He has always looked out for me since I started playing for Cardiff Blues, and he understands the ups and downs of what players go through. He always gives good advice and support when it's needed, and I think that comes from his experiences of playing professional rugby and managing players at Welsh regional level.

'Don't ever lose that self-belief,' he said to me. 'You have no reason to.' And I don't think I will lose it again. In fact, I'm sure I'll be stronger in the long term for that dark period I suffered early in 2013.

It had actually begun after the summer tour to Australia in 2012, if I look back with total honesty. I hadn't really been fit at the start of that three-Test series. We lost 3-0, although they were narrow defeats, especially the last two, but I felt I had been outplayed by my opposite number, David Pocock. I just didn't play as well as I can. I'd played well against him before, but he really did a number on me out there.

My form went on a downward spiral from there. I did have the odd good matches, such as those against New Zealand and Australia in the autumn series, but they took so much mental and emotional energy out of me. What was more, I had to do such a lot to get myself up for them that I was coming crashing back down afterwards.

There was a stage where I was at home thinking: 'It's not worth it. It's not worth going through all this stress.' Professional rugby was becoming too much. I remember being on the plane going to Dublin to play Leinster for the Cardiff Blues and I was looking at the man outside on the runway signalling the plane forwards and thinking: 'Why can't I have a job like that without any outside stress and pressure from others? Why do I put myself through this? If we lose again, I'm going to get slagged off – my parents and Rachel will be worrying themselves sick again.'

It was around this time that my dad decided he was going to leave Twitter. It wasn't about any personal abuse that he was getting, I think it was just that he was fed up with all the negativity that had been surrounding the team and me. He'd had enough of people forcing their negative opinions on him. My sister had quit Twitter for the same reasons during the autumn internationals. But he was not off there for long. I'm not sure he can stand life without being on there these days! He even got a sympathy tweet from Brian Moore. He was over the moon with that. And Holly was back on there before Christmas, too.

I was certainly in a bad place around the time of that France match, but then you come out the other side and you realise how much you enjoy the game. As I said, I think I have learnt so much from it. The problem was that I had bottled up all this negativity, and the only people I had told were Rachel and my parents. I was being asked questions about the Lions captaincy and it was so far from my mind it was unreal. All I wanted to do was get my form back and help Wales win the Six Nations. That was 90 per cent of my motivation in the last two games against Scotland and England, with, I suppose, 10 per cent thinking about Lions selection.

Wales's next match was against Italy, two weeks after the France match. It's usual for the team to be announced in the week of the match, but in this instance Rob Howley sprang a surprise by naming the team fully 11 days before the match. And it was the same starting team that had beaten France, which meant that I wasn't in it. I was on the bench, along with Alun-Wyn Jones, who was returning from a shoulder injury that he had suffered during the autumn internationals. This hardly helped my mood, but when Rob took me aside before the announcement, I fully understood his reasons for leaving me out.

The side had obviously won in France and had played awesomely well, and I was still not sure of my fitness because of the 'stinger' injury that forced me to miss that match. Rob wanted to have as much preparation time as possible before the Italy game, so it was a smart move to do what he did. I suppose he also wanted to avoid a lot of media speculation that there might have been about my position, both in the team and as captain.

But Ryan said some very kind words about me at this time, when there seemed to be an awful lot of negative stuff being said and written about me. He has always been someone for whom I have had the utmost respect. So it was very nice that he paid me that compliment at this particularly difficult time. 'You only ever look after the captaincy for someone else, and I would not have been hurt if I had not been named to lead the side in Rome,' he said. 'The issue for me was being picked in the team; the disappointment is always being left out.

'Sam is the squad captain and he is a kid with a bright, bright future. I have huge respect for him as a player, captain and bloke and cannot believe the reaction that has blown up over him. He will fight his way through this and, like a lot of the younger players in the squad, his career skyrocketed early on. They have all had to cope with the other side.

'The best players in the world have long careers by learning how to weather storms and not going to either end of the extreme in victory or defeat. I have been around a while and as an older guy I am coming to the table and betting all-in every time, not torturing myself mentally. What this Wales team has, and this was evident in the second half against Ireland, is heart. The players gave everything in Paris and the look on their faces at the end said it all for me.'

I was raring to go by the time of the Italy match. I knew I was fully fit because on the Monday before the match I survived a contact session with our fitness trainer Dan Baugh, the former Cardiff and Canada flanker. He is one tough man, and when he is wearing a 10kg-weighted vest he is even harder to tackle than usual. He just ran at me flat out for ten minutes and I had to keep tackling him. I survived. My shoulder was fine.

It was a strange situation for me, though, being on the bench. I was certainly more relaxed. I normally can't eat at all before a match but I could here, just as I had been able to when I was on the bench against Samoa in the autumn. I was able to take in the occasion more.

In terms of the captaincy, I just let Ryan take the reins. He is very good at that, but it wasn't as if I took a back seat. I would still speak up in training sessions if I felt that was right, just as I would have done if I was captain. Individually, all I could do was strip back everything in my game so that I could try to make a real impact if I got to come off the bench in Rome. I wanted to come on and help win the match, but I also wanted to do enough myself to get back in the team.

There were, of course, the inevitable questions about how this might affect my Lions chances, and especially the captaincy. As I've said, I was not thinking about that, but Rob Howley said publicly that it wouldn't harm them. 'Not at all,' he said when asked that question about the Lions. 'Although I think that is a question for Warren Gatland, not for me. But there have been many players not playing international rugby who have come into a Lions selection. So it is not a given that you have to be playing international rugby to go on a Lions tour, and it's not a given you have to be captain of your national team to be captain of the Lions.

'I have spoken to Sam and he understands that's the nature of sport. I am sure Sam will be an excellent captain in his career, but for this game we decided to go with same fifteen. The pressure on this side for Italy is the same as it was going to Paris.'

It wasn't just that I wasn't thinking about the Lions captaincy at this stage. I didn't even want to captain Wales. It was time for me to talk about it; I had to get it off my chest. So I spoke to Andy McCann about it before the Italy match. I told him that I was in the same situation as I had been two years earlier when I had told him that I didn't want to be Wales captain for the World Cup.

'I'm hating the captaincy again,' I said. I think it was partly because I didn't think I deserved it. It was strange because I always say to my mum and dad that they shouldn't be like those people who read and believe everything that is written in the papers, but during this period I ended up being one of those people. I couldn't help myself.

'I don't care what people think will happen regarding the Lions captaincy at the moment, I just need to get back playing well for Wales and enjoying it,' I said to Andy. That's no disrespect to the Lions; it's just the frame of mind I was in at the time. When we'd spoken about captaincy before the World Cup, I'd had to have a go at it really, but now here we were after I had captained Wales 19 times and I was still not enjoying it.

As it was, I got only about 12 minutes off the bench at the end in Rome. We won the match 26-9, a result with which we were delighted because the conditions were terrible and we had to change our game plan at the last minute to take them into account. It wasn't a fixture we wanted to play at all, with the ball in play for only about 35 minutes and lots of kicking, but in the circumstances we managed things well.

Happily, I was restored to the team at seven, instead of Justin Tipuric, for the next match against Scotland. I wasn't captain, however. Ryan was in charge again. Did I think I would be selected? Well, Cardiff Blues did actually play up in Glasgow during the weekend off between the Italy and Scotland matches, and when I was not released to play in that I did wonder whether I might be playing against Scotland. Having said that, it was always at the back of my mind that the same team that beat France and Italy might be picked again, which would have meant I was a replacement again.

Because of that, I was a little surprised when I was selected, but I was also delighted. Everybody wants to be in the starting XV. That has always been my motivation since I was a youngster – I have always wanted to wear the No 7 jersey of Wales. As I've said, it was a relief that I wasn't captain. After I had spoken to Andy McCann before the Italy game, we had decided to let things settle until after that game and then I would speak to Rob about the captaincy. When I had had doubts before the World Cup, it had been Andy who had first mentioned them to Warren Gatland. But I told Andy that I would speak to Rob about it now. The captaincy just felt like a huge burden. And I told my parents and Rachel how I felt.

I remember thinking that captaincy cannot be that bad before I became the captain, but, once you've experienced it, you realise how stressful it can be. If you're not having an 8/10 performance as captain, it seems that you are easily punished in the media if the team does not do well. But I did not have to speak to Rob. He came to me first and told me that, although I was in the team at seven for the Scotland match, Ryan was going to be captain. I immediately thought to myself: 'This is the dream scenario.'

I said to him: 'To be honest, mate, I was going to have a word with you anyway. I feel at the moment that I just need to drop the captaincy and get back to my old self as a player and a person. I want to be in the changing rooms before a game and just listen to my crazy music for an hour, not say a word and then go out and smash the opposition. That's how I approach my game best.'

I didn't want to worry about coin tosses, which way we should play, what I was going to say to the players before the game and at half time. I didn't want to do the press conference on a Thursday. I didn't want any of that stuff. I just wanted to go out there and be selfish – maybe in a team sport that is the wrong word to use – but at this time it felt like the right one. I thought if I played well, it would be best for the team.

Quite a bit was made of my being at the back of the press conference at our Vale of Glamorgan team hotel on the Tuesday before the match when Ryan and Rob spoke about the team announcement. But I was just there to see what was said, as I had to do some press duties afterwards. And I thought Rob said some really nice things about me and I thanked him for that afterwards. He was great to me through-out the Six Nations, keeping me informed of his thoughts and what he expected of me. At no point did he leave me in the dark.

He said to me that he had been stripped of the Wales

captaincy once when he was a player and, though he didn't believe it at the time, it was the best thing that happened to him in the end. His situation was obviously not quite the same as mine, but it did mean that we could empathise with each other on the subject. I felt I got closer to him during the tournament, because we were both very honest with each other.

At the time, however, I couldn't say what I really felt about the captaincy. So this is what I said to the press about the subject and about returning to the side. I still think it encapsulated my feelings and thoughts then: 'I wouldn't say it's a relief not to have the captaincy. Obviously, you want to keep it. It's a great honour to have. But the positive I can take out of it is I can really concentrate on myself and do everything I can to make sure I have a good game. Not being captain does allow me to completely focus on what I have to do and my role at the weekend.

'It makes it a bit easier for me to approach the game – I have one less thing to think about ... I can just fully focus on myself and what I have to do preparation-wise to enable me to play the best I can. From that point of view, it does help. Getting the captaincy back won't be a motivating factor. Maybe it could happen again and, if the opportunity came around again, you'd do it. But my focus right now is making sure I do myself justice and play well for the side on the weekend. It almost feels like winning my first cap again because of the need to impress. That feeling is really good. Not knowing whether you are going to be playing each week definitely puts you on edge more.'

I remember talking to Leigh Halfpenny once about how he had been dropped by Wales and that since then he has done absolutely everything – every single bit of extra training he can – to make sure that it doesn't happen again. That's how I felt before that Scotland game. I also recall Warren Gatland saying to us once that we should play every game for Wales as if it was our last. I'd got my place back and I never wanted to let go of it again.

I obviously knew that Justin Tipuric would be desperately trying to get that place back from me, but I have always liked that competition. It has always kept spurring me on. Some of the players were taking the mick a bit in training, saying things to me and Justin like: 'Shall I stand between you two?' But the truth was that we were always helping and supporting each other. We shared a room together in Rome for the Italy match and spent hours playing Fifa on our iPads and talking football. He's an Everton fan and, as is fairly well known now, I'm a Spurs supporter, so there was plenty of Premier League banter. I think we finished above them in the league, didn't we?

It was time to perform. I deliberately put a lot of pressure on myself during the week to do that. Rachel said that I was acting a little bit strangely and that she thought it was best to leave me alone. But I was still struggling with my confidence. So I did some work with Andy McCann on the Thursday and Friday before the match, and even on the morning of the game on the Saturday. I admitted to him on the Thursday: 'I have lost all my confidence. I just don't feel happy in myself. I am not the same person I was twelve months ago.'

It was quite a big admission to make at the time, but I felt I needed to do it. I needed to address my problems. So we talked. And I grew in confidence.

My first appearance in the Six Nations had been against Scotland as a replacement in 2010. It was a game we won 31-24, but it was also a match in which it was said that the Scotland back row had the better of the Welsh back row. So when Dan Lydiate and I were brought in to play in 2011, we were determined that that would not happen again. And I had had one of best games for Wales in that match up in Scotland, winning the man-of-the-match award and making probably one of my best tackles (on centre Nick de Luca), as we won 24-6. So there was no reason why I couldn't go into this game with a good deal of confidence.

Andy asked me what my target was for the match, and I told him that I wanted to get the man-of-the-match award and nothing less. He said to me: 'Yes, that's fine, but you might have a man-of-the-match performance, but the commentary people selecting it may not see it that way.'

'Well, I'm going to have that good a game that they can't ignore me,' I said. 'I have to be man of the match.' I knew that if I did that, then there might be a good chance that the team would win. I did get that award and, of course, we did win.

I went into the game with so much more confidence. Andy always gets me to go through my strengths in my mind before-hand. So I go through a jackal (where you compete for the ball on the floor after a tackle has been made), a tackle, a carry and a line-out win. I play them in my mind. Those are the things

I want to do in the first ten minutes. Those are the boxes I have to tick. If I do them then I am doing my job.

But it was not as if things went entirely smoothly. In the first half, I was solid without being outstanding. We were only 13-12 up at half time after Leigh Halfpenny's penalty had just put us ahead. I went in for that break thinking: 'I'm doing the same old thing again. I'm making my tackles and hitting rucks, but I am not making an impact.' It was quite literally at that stage where I thought: 'Sod this. I'm just going for it.'

I had to do something. Luckily for me Stuart Hogg, who became a Lions colleague later, provided me with an opportunity to do so early in the second half. He came running back at us on a counter-attack and I just lined him up for the tackle. It was a big hit and I drove him backwards before getting into position for the jackal. I managed to hold my position and get my hands on the ball and get a penalty against him for not releasing as four Scottish players came in to help.

I was back. As referee Craig Joubert blew his whistle for the penalty, and a lot of my colleagues tapped me in congratulation, I could feel myself grow. It might well have been the defining moment of my season. It might well have been the moment from which I began my rise to a Lions place. It meant that much to me. It was that important. I suddenly felt that I could do anything.

From then on, I was a different player. My speed into position at the breakdown was a lot quicker than it had been for a long time, and I eventually managed four turnovers in the match. That was even though our analyst Rhys Long had set me a pre-match target of five and he said afterwards that he wasn't happy, before breaking out into a big smile. It was definitely the best game I had had at the breakdown all season. I was pleased with how I had played against New Zealand during the autumn series, but this was even better. There might not have been too much from me in an attacking sense, but it just wasn't that type of game.

It's always the same against Scotland. The matches are always tough and they are also always hyped up as a big battle of the back rows. And this was no different. I knew that I would face a huge challenge up against Kelly Brown, their captain and seven. He is someone I have got to know a little bit off the field and get on really well with, having been to the RBS Six Nations launch with him before the start of the tournament, as well as the Rugby World Cup draw at the end of 2012.

But I felt I had won that battle, and we had won the war as a team. It might have been a bit of a scrappy match, with a lot of penalties especially at the scrummage, but we eventually won 28-18 to ensure that we had won five consecutive away matches in the Six Nations for the first time.

Andy McCann was in the changing room when we got back inside and I went up to him and gave him a huge hug. His work had paid off. I've said before how much I rate him, and this was just another example of his help working for me. I was quite emotional afterwards. Some jerseys you give away, but that Scotland one I will never give away because it meant so much to me.

If I'm honest, I wanted to stick two fingers up to my critics. There had been so many of them and I felt that the pressure that they had put on me was incredible. I did my post-match interview and then, as we were walking around the stadium to thank the fans, I saw my mum and dad in one corner. My dad looked as if he had been crying. I know they both go through exactly the same things as me. So I went over to them and gave them hugs. My dad was swearing and punching the air in delight. I think, like me, he was shouting at my critics. So as I walked off, I threw my man-of-the-match medal to them. I said they could keep it. It was a thank you to them for all their support. And I told them that again later when I met up with them.

I stayed with the boys to celebrate for about an hour, but then I really wanted to go to meet up with my parents. I just felt awesome. I knew I was ready to take on England the next week.

There was disappointment for Ryan Jones, though, who had had to go off after 48 minutes with a shoulder injury. Justin Tipuric had come on to replace him, and I said to him immediately: 'Let's go really hard at the breakdown for thirty minutes.'

We communicated really well at the rucks. Sometimes one of us would say: 'I'll go low and you compete for the ball,' and then vice versa. I got two penalties from Justin's low chop tackles and I also got two of my four turnovers while he was on. I thought we worked really well together.

I also took over as captain for those last 30 minutes or so

when Ryan went off, and I actually felt really comfortable being in charge during that time. I was pretty vocal, which quite a lot of people seemed to pick up on, because I was using the experience I had gained in some tight matches we had lost when I was captain, like my first game in charge against the Barbarians in the summer of 2011, and the many close fixtures we had had against Australia in 2012.

I was just making sure that everyone knew what they had to do in every situation in those last periods of the game. And I was also happy with the relationship I had with referee Craig Joubert. That was to prove important as he was to referee the Lions' second Test out in Australia and, as I said, Warren Gatland mentioned my relationship with referees when announcing me as Lions captain. Craig had refereed us quite a few times before, but I really felt that I could talk to him.

There was one occasion when I was penalised as I attempted a turnover. Basically, you must release the player you have tackled just for a split second before getting on your feet and jackaling over him. At this stage I wasn't always in the habit of doing what a few other players were doing at the time – England's Chris Robshaw was especially good at it – which was lifting my arm in the air to signify that I had released the player, before beginning to jackal. So when Craig penalised me, I asked him: 'Was that for unclear release?' He said yes. 'Do I need to release sooner?' Again he said yes. There was no problem, just good communication between the two of us. In the heat of the moment, it is easy to be too emotional and too aggressive towards the referee. I just try to stay as calm as I can and ask clear questions. I never query his decisions.

There was just one game left of the championship: England at home. Our hopes of a second successive Grand Slam had, of course, gone with defeat in that first match against Ireland, but there was still a chance of the championship. The problem was that England were still unbeaten. We had played Scotland on the Saturday and England took on Italy the next day at home, where it was assumed that they would stretch their points difference so that, even if we won in Cardiff, it might be difficult to take the title.

But there was a surprise in store. England beat Italy by just 18-11. I thought they would have won by 20 clear points at home. That's what I would have predicted beforehand, anyway. So, as I watched the game at home, I was pleasantly surprised by what I was seeing. Italy gave it a real thrash. In the end, I thought England defended really well in the final moments to keep Italy out.

It changed everything. I thought we might have been looking at having to win by about 16 points to take the championship. That would have been very difficult against England. Now it was only a margin of eight points to make it certain, or even just seven points and then tries would have to be taken into account. It was definitely doable. After all, we had beaten England by seven points at Twickenham in 2012 in what was the hardest game of our Grand Slam season.

The first piece of news, though, for this championship shoot-out (and, of course, a possibility of a Grand Slam for

England) in Cardiff was that Ryan was ruled out with his shoulder injury. I was gutted for him, because he had captained the side so well during the campaign, and he had been in good form, too. But that only clouded the captaincy issue further. If Ryan had been fit, he would have continued as captain and there would have been no awkward questions to answer. As I said, I knew Rob would ask me, but I politely turned it down. Rob and I then decided that we would not say that this was what had happened, rather that it had been a mutual decision. That way there would be less fuss. But I know it was not easy for Rob to explain when he was quizzed about it at the team announcement.

'The way Sam played last week against Scotland, he was man of the match, and he didn't really want to change that,' he said. 'I think it speaks volumes for Sam. One thing about our squad is how selfless they are. It would have been easy for him to say yes. He said he would rather stick to his preparation and had really enjoyed it [last week].'

So Rob was then asked whether I had turned the captaincy down. 'It was a conversation Sam and I had,' he said. 'I have gauged Sam over the last three or four weeks. He has been outstanding over the last few weeks when he hasn't been involved. As I've said over the last three weeks, it is about what is best for the Welsh team, playing against England on Saturday, and that situation is Gethin Jenkins to be captain.

'I think as a coach you have a gut feeling about a player and how he feels. As a coach you always take in his thoughts and considerations. The way Sam played against Scotland, I had a gut feeling I would rather he just focused on his own game. That is how I saw it as a coach. You have to make those difficult decisions when they come and that is in the best interests of this national team.'

I always thought Gethin Jenkins would do a great job, so it was not a problem. There was some talk about my not being captain, but there was nothing over the top and certainly nothing that was going to affect my preparation for the game. But with Ryan out (and I should mention that Dan Lydiate was missing for the whole tournament after breaking his ankle right at the start of the season), I was also going to wear the No 6 shirt for the first time for Wales, with Justin at seven.

It was something with which I was comfortable. The roles were always going be interchangeable at different situations throughout the game. And we, of course, had worked really well together against Ireland and Scotland. I was also very keen to impress in the No 6 jersey because my mate Dan was always going on about how he had won man of the match in the seven jersey against Fiji in 2010. But the truth was that we were all keen to impress. This was the championship decider and the last international before the Lions squad was going to be selected. Matches don't come much bigger. Well, maybe a Lions Test, but we will come to that later.

I was so excited. This was simply one of those special games you play in. I heard Ryan saying that it was the sort of occasion you will always remember playing in, and that proved to be so true. I will never forget what happened.

On the bus on the way to the ground we were shown a

short motivational video just before we turned into Westgate Street alongside the Millennium Stadium. It ended with the message: 'Our Trophy, Our Stadium.' That stuck in everyone's minds, and then we walked into the dressing room to see the trophy itself sitting there on a table in the middle of the room. That was a surprise, but again the message was strong and powerful. We realised: 'That is ours and England are coming here to try to take it off us in our back yard.' We would do everything to ensure that didn't happen.

Once we ran out on to the pitch the atmosphere in the stadium was quite incredible. And the singing of the anthem was the most emotional I have ever known. It honestly took everything to hold it together at that point. I just felt so proud to be playing for that team in front of that crowd. I remember thinking: 'If I was an English player who has never played here before, I'd be pretty shocked by all this.' It was that charged, that emotional.

We have a saying in the Wales team: 'Empty the tank.' In other words, make sure you don't leave anything left, and give your all on the pitch. I certainly did that in this game. There was a moment just before 70 minutes was up on the clock when I sank to my knees. The physio came running on thinking I was injured, but I soon assured him that I wasn't. I just needed a breather. I could barely take my shirt off after the game.

But it was worth it: we won by 30-3. It still makes me smile now when I write that scoreline. It was unbelievable in many ways. I had always believed that we could win by the seven or eight points required to win the championship, but to win by 27 was not something that anyone had seen coming. It was quite ruthless, really. We thought that we could dominate England physically, firstly at the scrummage and then at every contact area, and I think we did that. Not that it was easy, of course. Every time you play against England, you wake up the next morning feeling as if you have been hit by a bus, and this was no different. We never let our feet off the pedal at any stage. Everybody seemed to have their best game of the tournament, from the front row where the scrummage went quite brilliantly to Leigh Halfpenny at the back, who ended up being man of the tournament.

I thought Justin Tipuric and I worked really well together again and, with Gethin as good over the ball as any seven in the northern hemisphere, it was like we had three sevens, which must have been difficult to deal with. As the game opened up in the second half, Justin came into his own, playing like an old-school seven, just like, say, Martyn Williams.

It was a real team performance of special intensity and physicality. And in front of Warren Gatland, who was ready to pick his Lions squad, too. It's funny how the little things sometimes matter. It was one small incident in the first half that Warren then mentioned when announcing me as Lions captain.

Referee Steve Walsh had penalised me at a breakdown when Ian Evans tackled Brad Barritt and I was the first man there. Walsh thought I had gone beyond the ball before being 'dragged' back onto Barritt. I didn't agree, of course, and wanted clarification from Walsh. I wasn't captain and you are not really allowed to speak to the referee unless you are captain, but I felt I had a good enough relationship with him to do so.

So I did speak to him. 'You went beyond the ball,' he said in response. I made sure I didn't do that again. Walsh received quite a lot of criticism afterwards – especially from England supporters, of course! – but I thought he was very consistent. Our scrummage was dominant and we put a lot of pressure on the English ball at the breakdown, and I think we were rewarded for that.

There was also a moment in the changing room at half time that Leigh very kindly mentioned to the press afterwards. It wasn't something I thought too much of the time, but it clearly had an effect on Leigh, which was nice to hear. 'Gethin spoke first and then Sam spoke up and asked how much did we want to win it more than England,' Leigh said. 'He told us that whenever we were shattered or felt like we didn't have anything left to give, just to think of that feeling of us lifting the trophy again. They were incredible words and inspired us all. He wasn't captain for that day, but as soon as he spoke up I thought about his words during the second half.'

Thanks, Pence! There was me thinking that I could not make inspirational speeches. Mind you, Leigh is a very emotional man.

I must admit it was the most special game in which I have been involved for Wales, because it was such a complete performance by the side at a crucial time. It was an even better feeling than winning the Grand Slam against France in 2012.

After that game I lifted the Six Nations trophy, but I hadn't played the whole game because of injury. Indeed, I had played only two full games in the tournament. In 2013, I played three full games and I felt like I contributed a lot more. I felt that I deserved my place up on the podium after beating England.

So when Ryan and Gethin went up to collect the trophy, I was bouncing up and down like a kid. I didn't do that in 2012. Despite it not being a Grand Slam, to beat England at home in the manner we did was more satisfying than the Grand Slam. The lights were turned off in the stadium and we were called up one by one to receive our medals. It was brilliant, and the crowd were going mad. But we had known in the build-up it would be like that. There was just so much interest, support and enthusiasm that it felt like a bigger finale than the Grand Slam. The Welsh are rather passionate about playing England after all.

I stood next to Leigh, which was great. We have come through the system together. I felt so happy. I felt worthy of being there. I was so relieved. I was screaming my head off. I got a really big cheer when I went up. The whole experience left me close to breaking down because I was so happy. Walking around the ground with my winner's medal is something I shall never forget. The noise coming back from the crowd was immense. I felt like a rock star. And I've always wanted to be one of them!

I began to think back over what had happened and take in all the action. At six I knew that I had to play a slightly different role. You have to do much more ball-carrying there and I knew beforehand that I had to step up in that regard. I had put myself under a lot of pressure to do so before the game, and had worked with Andy McCann on that, especially in terms of visualisation exercises, because it is a part of my game I am constantly working on.

Of course, I was particularly pleased with the break I made in the second half that led to Alex Cuthbert's second try in the match. Because I have been so focused on the breakdown in recent years, I haven't made a break like that since I was a kid. It was a sneaky pick-and-go from a position I normally wouldn't consider doing that from. Toby Faletau had initially run from inside our 22 and I just went in to seal the ball. But then I noticed that England had left nobody behind the ruck except the replacement scrum-half Danny Care, so I picked and went.

Suddenly I was clear and hurtling upfield. A few things were going through my mind as I approached the last defender, Owen Farrell. 'Do I side step? Do I just keep running into him? Or do I kick?' I wish now that I'd kicked, but I did keep running, and I was tackled. But we did eventually score from the break anyway.

One thing I did not realise until after I watched the game back afterwards was all the hype concerning me and Chris Robshaw. I honestly had no idea that there was so much talk about us competing for the same position in the Lions squad and for the Lions captaincy. Watching the game again, it was obvious that battle was a huge talking point, even if we weren't in direct opposition. Of course, Chris did not make the Lions squad in the end, but I thought it was a really nice touch that he sent me a message after the squad announcement to say well done and good luck. He has the same agent as George North and he texted George to pass on his best wishes. I thought that was very classy of him.

So there were about 79 minutes of the match gone and I found myself sitting on the replacements' bench with Gethin Jenkins, and he said: 'What are we going to do about this trophy?' I said that Ryan, who had been captain in three games, had to go up to collect it. 'Maybe we can stand either side of him,' said Gethin. But then later we were told that only two players could go up. Even though I had captained during this campaign, it had to be Ryan and Gethin.

I was happy with that, and I was happy enough to have a couple of drinks after the match, my first since last July! There was an after-match function at the Hilton Hotel and then we headed into Cardiff with our wives and partners. But, as you can imagine, it was rather chaotic. By 12.30am, I was on the team bus back to our team hotel out in the Vale of Glamorgan. I was actually surprised to see so many of the team back there, but it had been a draining day. I had almost fallen asleep during the after-match dinner through sheer exhaustion.

We spent a few hours in the bar there celebrating, with our medals around our necks. And there may even have been the odd word said about the Lions, for that time had come. The match against England had been the audition, there was no escaping that fact, and we had all put on a pretty good show.

3

Departure Time

This was it at last: 27 May 2013. After all the build-up, the British and Irish Lions tour began with a flight to Hong Kong for the first match of the tour, against the Barbarians. I must admit that I surprised myself a little – I was so relaxed about it all. My parents, my brother and my fiancée Rachel said that they had never seen me so relaxed about a rugby experience. That was because ever since I had been appointed captain of the tour I had been thinking to myself: 'Just enjoy it and give your all on and off the field.' I desperately wanted to win the series, of course, but I was just really looking forward to getting out there, first to Hong Kong and then to Australia, and enjoying it. I really couldn't wait.

Before I left for the tour, I had got together with Andy McCann and we went to what I call my 'happy place' up in the woods near my home in Rhiwbina. It's where I go to reflect, usually taking the family dogs with me. It overlooks the whole of Cardiff and the bay, and I can see the Millennium Stadium from there. I like to contrast the feelings I have on a match day, when I am playing in the stadium, with how I feel on that bench. There are probably only about five miles between the two places, but the contrast between the nerves and emotion of a match day and the tranquility of that bench up in the woods could not be greater. It's such a nice place to go. And I go there often. Indeed, I went up there on the day I got back from this Lions tour to reflect on what I'd been through.

Anyway, Andy and I sat down on the bench there. It was a little strange, because I hadn't been there with anyone else before. It was usually only me and my thoughts. But this time we did an exercise to help me switch off. Andy told me to shut my eyes, do the controlled breathing techniques that we have practised many times before, and then to relax. He wanted me to clear my mind completely, and then he would time me until I said that something had come into my mind, whether it was about rugby or whatever else.

The first time I tried it, I managed about five seconds. But after practising it quite a few times I was able to manage about two minutes, and in that time I was totally relaxed, just taking in the peace and calm of the woods, hearing only the noise of the birds and feeling the breeze. I took a photo of the view, and Andy took a picture of me with the view in front of me. I kept them on my phone and Andy told me that whenever I felt under stress on tour to look at these photos and then take my mind back to the woods so that I could relax. I did that a few times when I could find some privacy and it really worked.

People had been saying to me in the weeks since the squad announcement: 'Wow, being captain of the Lions is such a massive thing!' And, yes, it is the greatest honour a rugby union player in Britain and Ireland can receive. That really hit home when we were at our first training camp, at the Vale Resort in Cardiff, and among the many messages of congratulation I received there was a lovely card delivered to my room there. It was in beautiful handwriting and the message was heartfelt. At the bottom it was signed 'Phil Bennett'. I thought that was such a nice touch from him, the last Welsh player to be named a Lions tour captain, back in 1977. That he had made such an effort to do that made me both proud, as well as acutely aware of how big a deal this was. I've made sure I have kept that card.

My family had also given me a brilliant send-off before I went, organising a special celebration meal at my favourite restaurant, the Juboraj in Rhiwbina. I love that place. Every time I come home from a tour, you can guarantee that I will be there within one or two nights of returning. Going there is always something I look forward to when I am away. My parents organised it with Ana Miah, who is the Juboraj group director. There is a room at the back of the restaurant and Ana said that my parents could invite 30 members of the family, while he would invite 20 guests of his own, who turned out to be his most regular customers.

I turned up and I saw Steve Williams, who was one of my teachers at Whitchurch High School in Cardiff. I said to him: 'What a coincidence, Steve. I have to apologise if your food is a bit late because there are about fifty of us having a bit of a party out the back.'

I went into the party and there was an overhead projector with a picture of me in my Lions kit and a good luck message on it. Steve came and sat down next to me. I thought: 'This is a bit embarrassing. What's he doing sitting here?' That's not meant as any offence to Steve, who was in charge of the first team rugby at Whitchurch, and to whom I owe an awful lot, but I just thought it was a family party and I didn't expect to see anyone else there.

Then Ana said to me: 'I've invited Steve along to make a speech.' I apologised to Steve then, but he knew it was a surprise thing so there was certainly no awkwardness. And when Steve spoke, he did so really well, talking for about 15 minutes about my schooldays. It got me going a bit, if I am honest. It was quite emotional. Then Ana spoke and said how proud he was to have me there as a Rhiwbina boy. And he presented me with a specially commissioned portrait by Dan Peterson, a well-known illustrator from Cardiff. By coincidence, it was drawn from a picture of me during the national anthem, which both Andy McCann and myself really like, because it shows me being really focused.

At this point I started thinking I was going to have to say something. I'd said to my dad beforehand that I wanted to do this party at the Juboraj, but I didn't want to have to speak. I often say that because I don't particularly like speaking in public. But this had been the Sam Warburton show for 20 minutes and everybody had been so kind to me. Ana asked me if I would like to say anything.

I had to speak, but could I? I was getting very emotional.

This was no normal audience – it consisted mainly of my family. I stood up and everyone cheered. They then went silent and I lost it. I put my hands over my face and I think everyone thought I was joking, so they all laughed. But I wasn't. I was struggling here.

I said out loud: 'Andy McCann. Deep, controlled breathing. Compose yourself.' That's something I do quite often in games. Again, everyone giggled because they thought I was joking, but I still wasn't. I was doing my utmost not to break down when I said simply: 'Just a normal kid from Rhiwbina who picked up a rugby ball and did decent.' This was an incredibly emotional moment for me. I walked back to my parents and Rachel, who were all so proud of me and blubbing by this time!

It was another reminder of how important a job this was and also of how proud my family were of me. I really appreciated their support and the very kind leaving party. I was still relaxed at the prospect of being Lions captain, but this family affair was just a little bit too emotional at the time.

Mentally, I had to prepare myself for the Lions captaincy just as I did for the Wales captaincy. With Wales, it's about bringing four regions together, and often when you go into camp you don't know some of the players that well. With the Lions, it was about bringing four countries together. It was the same process, admittedly on a bigger scale, of course, but the fundamentals remained the same. That was how I was tackling it.

I thought a lot of people were trying to complicate the captaincy, with the questions they were asking about it before

I left. I always thought the players from each of the countries would bond naturally. That's what rugby players do, and especially when you know that they are going to be so proud to be representing the Lions. Obviously, it will always take a little time for players to get to know each other, especially in the first week of a tour where you will always stay close to those you know best, because that is where you feel most comfortable.

I can honestly say that on this tour there were no problems in this regard. The players bonded. There were not any divisions. This was actually another of the potential scenarios Andy McCann and I had talked about beforehand, and it was another problem I was not to face. It simply didn't happen.

Yes, there have been stories of divisions on past tours, but that was not the case here. I remember speaking to Paul O'Connell during the tour and he remarked on how good the spirit and morale was. Of course, there was some gentle mickey-taking about cliques. There were six Leicester players (Tom and Ben Youngs, Manu Tuilagi, Geoff Parling, Dan Cole and Tom Croft) on tour, so they often got some stick for being in a clique. Tom Youngs and Dan Cole were obviously good mates and spent a lot of time together, but then so do Dan Lydiate and I.

At one stage Andy Farrell said to us: 'I'd heard you two were close mates, but I didn't realise how close!' It did get me thinking that I should perhaps be careful about spending too much time with Dan. For instance, whenever we do a gym session with Wales, it's almost second nature that we walk in and just nod to each other and then crack on with working together. So there were a few instances where I made a conscious decision not to train with Dan in the gym, and chose different partners. Paul O'Connell ended up being one of them quite often.

This was all part of the leadership compass I had developed with Andy McCann. Three directions of it ('professional attitude', 'positive attitude' and 'leading by example') I found relatively easy to implement, but it is always the fourth – 'developing relationships with players' – that I find I have to work on. So this was just an example of that. For example, when I walked in to dinner and saw three huge tables of players, and I would make sure that I chose the one with the fewest Welsh players on it so that I could get to know the others more quickly.

We had had two excellent training camps in Cardiff and Dublin before we left. Not everyone was present because of club commitments – there were the two domestic finals of the Aviva Premiership and the RaboDirect Pro12 just two days before we flew – but there was no way we were going to be using that as an excuse ahead of our first game against the Barbarians in Hong Kong on 1 June.

As I said to the press at the time: 'I think we should be quite well prepared for the Barbarians game. Preparation won't be an excuse as we will have had three weeks together before kick-off and the Baa Baas will have had less preparation time than us. The schedule from a Lions point of view could be better, but we have just got to deal with what we've got at the moment. We've still got good numbers in training, so there are still plenty of options. Ahead of the autumn internationals and Six Nations with Wales, we only have two weeks' prep anyway.'

The first camp was from 14 to 17 May at the Vale Resort base we use with Wales. It was great to get down to some work together at last. The boys gelled really quickly, as I thought and hoped they would. And immediately you could see that this was something very different. This was a notch up from our normal international stuff. Even just lifting weights and doing fitness work, you could tell people were lifting their standards from international level. Excuse the pun, but the bar was raised straight away, as all the boys were trying to make a statement to secure those Test spots immediately.

Warren Gatland emphasised to us from the start that he felt he had a squad where everyone could compete for a Test starting XV place, and that is always the best way to be, so that everyone is on edge in training.

'You don't want to become complacent and think you have got a starting place in the team,' I said to the press. 'I like it when you go into the team announcements and you are on the edge not knowing if you are going to get picked. Knowing that you might not be involved is what keeps you going in training and keeps you dedicated off the pitch as well.'

Warren's positive attitude was already in evidence. 'He is extremely optimistic, as all Kiwis are, and that's what I am like myself, and I think his confidence rubs off on the players,' I said.

Departure Time

From the minute we first met up, we were all just looking forward to getting on the training pitch, getting the ball in our hands and getting prepared for that first game against the Barbarians. 'The opportunity will pass you by if you don't embrace it,' I said. 'The players are really knuckling down. There is a lot of onus on them to make sure they learn the calls, whether it's in the team-room, on the laptops, so when you get to training you make sure you can do the business and make sure you get it all done in one go. Players are trying to learn very quick and are working extremely hard to get things right straight away, as time isn't really on our side. From my point of view, it's been great to see the players in training, and off the pitch as well, being so dedicated and learning the calls and picking things up so quickly.'

I was enjoying getting to know some of the players much better. I shared a room with Paul O'Connell in Cardiff. That was clearly a deliberate move by the management to put me with the captain of the 2009 tour to South Africa. Those rooming arrangements obviously helped interaction between players from different countries. I also shared with Owen Farrell, Tommy Bowe, Matt Stevens (twice), Jamie Heaslip and Leigh Halfpenny, as well as my mate Dan Lydiate, with whom I usually share when playing for Wales.

For Paul and me, it was just a case of us both getting to know each other at first. We were not necessarily talking about captaincy, just about our lives and our families, that sort of thing. Having played against him, my impression was that he would be quite a serious guy, as that's the way he comes across on the pitch. He is obviously a natural leader and a highly motivated one at that. But what I found when I got to know him better was that he is actually quite chilled out as a character, with a really good sense of humour. It became quite clear very quickly that he was one of the most popular characters in the squad.

When it was time for training, that was when he got serious. If you were to ask me now about the things I learnt from this Lions tour, one of the most striking things I would say was how professional Paul O'Connell is. He was undoubtedly one of the best trainers. Some players when they pass 30 look after their bodies a bit more in terms of workload and make sure they do not do too much. Not Paulie. He was always first in the gym and last to leave. As Dan Lydiate and I have similar attitudes, it was often the three of us who ended up training together. And, as I've mentioned, I often chose Paul as a partner when we were doing team gym sessions. It was a great experience.

As the tour went on, Paul's help with the captaincy was invaluable. I actually think that was one of the primary reasons why I enjoyed doing the job so much. He took so much weight off my shoulders. He showed those leadership qualities immediately during the training in Cardiff, even if it was just chatting to players in training at the end of sessions or if I was going to speak to the lads, he might say: 'I think you should say this . . .' For me, that was a great help.

I always welcome that sort of support from any player. And he was so good to have around in that regard. Sometimes, after he'd spoken to the players with some motivational words at the end of a session, he would say to me: 'Sorry, mate. I didn't mean to steal your thunder. You make sure you speak now.'

I'd reply: 'No, it's fine. That was brilliant.' He said that was how he and Brian O'Driscoll worked together with Ireland, helping each other out with the leadership role. And that's certainly what he did with me – as did Brian, of course. He was always helping me, and gave me nothing but support.

While we were in Cardiff I decided that we should start organising some of the committees that would help the squad function off the field during our time in Hong Kong and Australia. They certainly helped the bonding between players from the four countries. It's something most nations do on tour. Myself and a player from each of the nations all got together and we sat down and figured out a few committees, whether it was for entertainment, music, fines – all those sorts of things – just to keep things ticking along off the pitch and on the field as well.

I met up with Paul, Adam Jones, Richie Gray and Owen Farrell (it was going to be Matt Stevens, but for some reason I couldn't find him at the time) and asked them for recommendations for players who might fit the various roles on the committees. Those committees obviously couldn't come into full force until everybody was together, but we did manage to put certain things in place. It was hilarious hearing what each of them thought about their fellow countrymen and who might fit certain positions.

One appointment we didn't have to talk about was that of Stuart Hogg as the custodian of 'Bil', our Lion mascot, and a replacement for the previous mascot 'Leo', who had apparently become a bit too tatty. Charlie McEwen, the Lions' director of sales and marketing, had apparently found Bil in a toy shop at Geneva airport after a lot of searching. He was hunting for something that looked suitably fierce, rather than just some cuddly toy.

The responsibility of looking after the mascot always falls to the youngest member of the squad and everyone found it rather amusing when Stuart, who suffers quite badly from hay fever, started complaining that the lion's mane was making him itch and his eyes swell up!

We all also found it just as funny trying to hide Bil, so that Stuart might get fined. He was really panicking when he couldn't find it after training one day in Cardiff. He'd left it on some jumping blocks and it took him about half an hour to track it down afterwards. Talk about panic!

The announcers on the team bus were to be Sean O'Brien and Ian Evans, who are both very funny men. And the tour guides were named as Mike Phillips and Dan Cole. Every city we visited, they had to tell us something interesting about it. Dan is very well read and he delighted in giving us lots of highbrow educational information, which none of us found interesting, but he just carried on with it, knowing that it would raise a laugh and he would be shouted down. It was actually very amusing.

Phillsy threatened to do his first guide in French, but he didn't. He just acted arrogantly most of the time, which he isn't, but he quite likes being so just to be funny. So when we got to Melbourne later in the tour, he said to us one morning on the bus: 'I don't know if you know, but Kylie Minogue is from here. There is a rumour that we once went out together. It was huge global news at the time, and Kylie was asked by a reporter: "Is it right that you go out with Mike Phillips, the international rugby superstar?" To which Kylie replied: "I should be so lucky, lucky, lucky, lucky . . ."'

Now that did go down well! Other appointments for committees included Dan Lydiate, Richie Gray and Leigh Halfpenny being in charge of rooming arrangements. George North was in charge of laundry. And Toby Faletau, Manu Tuilagi and Mako Vunipola all had to share telling a joke of the day. The idea behind that was that they are all so quiet we wanted to get them to speak up a bit more. Poor Toby had said to me beforehand: 'Please don't get me to do anything where I have to speak.' I had to tell him I was outvoted! I have to say they were all terrible. Only Mako told the odd joke that was at all funny. No matter. I think they didn't mind. It was all in good humour.

There was also a music committee and it will probably be no surprise to you to learn that Matt Stevens was in charge of that. He was on *Celebrity X-Factor* – the Battle of the Stars – in 2006, after all. He reached the final, too. So he would often lead the singing (although Sean O'Brien was also pretty good – and funny! – with his Irish songs), especially on the bus journey we had from Newcastle to Sydney after we had played the Combined New South Wales and Queensland Country team and before we played the New South Wales Waratahs.

Throughout the tour on the bus, we were working on a lot of songs as a group – Oasis's 'Wonderwall' was one favourite (it had also been the 1997 Lions tour song, too) – but the one that became the main tour song was Mumford & Sons' 'Little Lion Man'. We always sang that after we had won.

The most important of them all was the fines committee. We decided that Rob Kearney should be head of that one, with Geoff Parling, Richard Hibbard and Conor Murray alongside him. They were savage, they really were. They were all on the lookout for any minor indiscretion, such as lateness, wrong clothing – those sorts of things. They wanted people to help them out by snitching, but you had to be careful doing that. I left the line-out calls on a table in one of the hotel rooms, and analyst Rhys Long picked them up afterwards to save any embarrassment.

So we were sitting next to each other on the bus soon afterwards when Rob Kearney came along. Rhys took great delight in telling Rob the story of what had happened, thinking I would cop a huge fine. But as he walked away, I saw Rob writing on his notepad: 'Rhys Long. Snitching . . .'

If we were fined, we then had to roll a dice to determine what our forfeit would be. For instance, at one stage if you rolled a number one, then you would just have to be a coffee boy for the day. That was probably the kindest of them, though. Poor Jamie Roberts had to down three pints of milk at one stage. Try doing that! If you rolled a six, you could be in serious trouble, as Charlie McEwen found out when he had to shave his head. At one meeting, if you rolled a three you had to take part in a dance-off. That was more attractive to some than others.

To Mike Phillips and Stuart Hogg it was no fun when they rolled threes. They were told that they had to do their dancing in the Business Lounge at Perth airport, just before we were due to fly from there to Brisbane for our third match of the tour, against the Queensland Reds. They were dreading it. Also down to dance was Dan Lydiate. Everyone thought he was dreading it too, but on the way there in the bus he'd said quietly to me how much he was looking forward to it. He just hadn't told anyone how much he enjoyed it. Or how good he was!

So there we all were at the airport and we gathered round to watch Phillsy and Hoggy begin dancing. They were awful! It was some of the worst dancing you will ever see. Phillsy was trying really hard, pretending to pull himself in on a rope, doing the 'worm', all that sort of stuff. But it just wasn't happening. Then suddenly a really good beat song came on – I think it was the Jason Nevis vs Run DMC 'It's Just Like That' – and Dan appeared. He was unbelievable. He completely wiped the floor with the others. He could do the shuffle, the moonwalk, body pop – he could do everything. He brought the place down. Everyone roared with laughter and cheered. I was videoing it on my phone, but I was laughing so much that I dropped it.

Dan was not the only performer, of course. When a new player joined the tour he had to sing a song at the front of the bus. So when prop Alex Corbisiero was called up from

England's tour of Argentina, after Cian Healy was injured in the second match (the first in Australia) against Western Force in Perth, he had to do it. And the following week after the match against Queensland Reds, Ireland's Simon Zebo joined us to cover for Tommy Bowe who had broken his hand in that match (although he stayed on tour and eventually ended up playing again). Scotland's prop Ryan Grant was also summoned to replace Gethin Jenkins, whose calf injury sadly ruled him out.

That was tough seeing players being ruled out. I had been keen to play alongside Cian because he has always impressed me. He's a very big unit, and so aggressive. And I've obviously played a lot alongside Gethin, so I was gutted for him. But it was great news for Tommy that he was able to stay after it was initially thought that he might be out of the tour, and a good boost for everyone because we thought that he was such a massive player for us.

With all due respect to Ryan, it was Corbs and Zeebs who stole the show in terms of entertainment. Corbs went to the front of the bus and Sean O'Brien as announcer was really ripping into him. Corbs was born in New York, and quite a lot of his family still live there, so Sean was calling him a big fat pizza boy and that sort of stuff. So Corbs did an off-the-cuff rap in which he totally destroyed Sean. It was quite brilliant, and the boys loved it.

Zeebs is brilliant at rapping, too, and so there was only one thing for it at some stage: he and Corbs had to have a rap-off! That was superb, too. It was like something out of the

Eminem film, *Eight Mile*. Zeebs can beatbox as well, as can Sean Maitland, so those three often formed an act for us on the bus.

Our second training camp before we left was held at Carton House in County Kildare from 20 to 24 May. 'It's been great. Training has run really smoothly,' I said about our work there. 'It's been a very hard-working group. Maybe that's because it's quite a young squad in general, but it's been very enjoyable. Everybody has had a great time in the last week and they were looking forward to getting back together after having the weekend off. I think we've made a lot of progress, because we've done quite a lot of organisational and conditioning work.'

Looking ahead to the tour, I said: 'Momentum is key. There might be setbacks on the tour, but it is about not panicking if they happen. As long as we learn from them and put things right for the next game, it is a good learning curve. I have been very impressed with the Australian sides in the Super Rugby tournament this year. The key players seem to be playing very well at the right time. Every time there is a Lions tour, the national side we are playing against – whether it is Australia, New Zealand or South Africa – always seem to come good in a Lions year, which shows how much it means to them.

'But it's been good. Speaking to some of the players that have been on tour before, it's a bit quieter than maybe past tours, when it comes to your characters that people are looking out for on the DVD. We've got a day off out here this week, so we'll plan something then to do as a squad, what exactly I'm not sure. There are a few nice golf courses around here and I know players like to play golf. We'll sit down and figure that out. When we all get on that plane, and we're in Australia for the first time as a full thirty-seven and management, I think that's when players might start to get quite excited, when you actually get abroad.'

My comments reflected the fact that it was a little quiet in those opening days. We sat around big tables for dinner and there would not be much noise at all. It got to the stage where some of the boys were saying sarcastically: 'There's a lot of good chat around here!' And there obviously wasn't.

I must admit that I was a tiny bit concerned at this stage and did consider trying to do something to bring the players closer together. I spoke to team manager Andy Irvine about it, and he said: 'As soon as we get to Hong Kong and we are actually abroad together as a full squad, we will be fine.' And he was right. Because we were then preparing for matches, players started helping each other more in sessions and in the analysis room.

I was sharing a room with Owen Farrell in Ireland, but it was with Mako Vunipola that I had to do what was called the 'Host the Pride' promotion in Ireland. Six players had had to do this while we were in Wales, and now another six of us (drawn randomly) had to do it in Ireland. Basically, what we had to do was go in pairs to have dinner with a family who had won this as a prize in a competition.

So Mako and I went to the house of Martin and Doreen Doyle and had a very enjoyable evening. Sean Maitland and

Departure Time

Leigh Halfpenny went together to visit another family, as did Richard Hibbard and Conor Murray to another place nearby. The six who had done this in Wales had been Toby Faletau, Ian Evans, Alex Cuthbert, Jonathan Davies, Adam Jones and Stuart Hogg. Mind you, Cuthie and Foxy (Jon Davies) were a little surprised to be greeted by two ladies dressed in England rugby shirts, who proceeded to give them quite a bit of stick all night!

The night before we left for Australia, we attended a farewell dinner at the Royal Courts of Justice in London. It was a glitzy red-carpet do, celebrating 125 years of Lions rugby as well as our own departure. And this was the first occasion on which I really felt I was leading the Lions, all of them (well, Rory Best wasn't there because he had only been called up that day, after Dylan Hartley had been banned for being sent off in the Aviva Premiership final). Now we were about to be welcomed up on stage, and I was standing there, holding Bil the mascot.

I looked behind me at all the boys in their Lions suits and what I saw was all these legends of rugby. It made me so proud to be leading them, and it made me realise how lucky I was to be there. Here I was in this hugely privileged position, a lad who had begun playing rugby at Rhiwbina in Cardiff. I began thinking of that club and all the other clubs in Cardiff, and then of all the other clubs in the county, then in Wales, then in England, Scotland and Ireland. Then, spread that over the age groups for about ten years, and I had been picked to captain a side from all those players, who would all doubtless love to play for the Lions. It really made me think. It was rather strange, but it made me very proud. It is the pinnacle, as some say, the SAS of rugby.

Sky Sports' Alex Payne was again doing the hosting and he conducted a short question-and-answer session with me, Warren Gatland and Graham Rowntree. 'Since the announcement, it has all been about having a successful tour and making sure we win,' I said to him and the large assembled audience of sponsors and friends in the Great Hall. 'Nobody among our players has got that in their CV – a Test-series win as a Lions player. That is absolutely everything. We are desperate to achieve that, and I know every player feels exactly the same way.'

We were staying that night at a hotel in Kensington, and before the dinner I had got into one of the lifts there with a couple of other players only to see a bloke dressed in running gear and with his head down. I couldn't believe my eyes. It was Matt LeBlanc, the actor who plays Joey in the sitcom *Friends*. I was star-struck. I absolutely love watching the series, and LeBlanc is probably my favourite TV personality alongside Will Smith. It's usually so obvious when someone recognises a famous person, so I was determined to play it cool. But there I was standing shoulder to shoulder with Matt LeBlanc.

I was so desperate to ask him for a photo, but I was just too shy to do so. It was the same when the James Bond actor Daniel Craig came into the dressing room after the final Test in Sydney at the end of the tour. I think I was about the only player who did not have a photo with him.

In fact the one I really wanted a photo with at some stage of the tour was Dr James Robson, our head doctor. I kept telling him he was a legend virtually every time I saw him. That's because it was his sixth tour and he had been on the 1997 tour to South Africa when the first tour video had been made. I was only eight then and rather impressionable! I so wanted a photo, but again was probably too shy to ask.

Anyway, LeBlanc left the lift and I couldn't stop laughing. I couldn't believe what had just happened. I immediately phoned Rachel to tell her, because she is a huge fan too, and she asked straight away: 'Did you get a photo?' She wasn't happy when I told her that I hadn't! I phoned my brother and sister immediately to tell them as well. I was seriously excited, and star-struck!

I was just as excited once we boarded the plane at Heathrow, bound for Hong Kong. The Lions hadn't won a Test series since that one in 1997 that I've just mentioned. There was going to be plenty of fun, some of which I have already spoken about, but the reality of the trip was that we were going to Australia (via Hong Kong) to win. In any sport I have ever played, it has always been about the winning. That is what I desperately wanted to do there.

So I have to admit that there was some initial disappoint-ment in Hong Kong. And I'm not talking about a knee injury I had picked up. We'll come to that in a minute. No, there was an incident on the Tuesday night that angered me a bit. I'm not going to name any names because I would never do that, but we went out as a squad that night and things started to get a little out of hand. I thought to myself: 'Some of the boys are going to get pissed here.' I knew that among them were players who were going to be in action in the first match against the Barbarians on the Saturday. I know that's what the Barbarians normally do, even if they were talking about an alcohol ban during this week, but that is no excuse in my opinion.

I didn't say anything that night, because I didn't want to be seen as a party-pooper, but tour manager Andy Irvine and Warren Gatland spoke with me the next day. They both knew what had happened, and I told them my opinion was: 'I think we should approach the Lions tour games just like the Olympics. It only happens every four years and for those fortunate enough to get picked, they should treat it with the same professionalism. Do you think Jess Ennis would drink less than a week before her eight hundred metres event?'

I rarely drink, and it's not that I think that rugby players should not drink at all – far from it – it's just that I think there is a time and a place for doing that. And this was not it, in my view. I told Gats that I thought it was unacceptable, and he said to me that he had given the boys some leeway to see how they had behaved. He was not impressed. I definitely think he bore in mind what happened that night as the tour went on.

As for my knee injury, I had felt some pain during training in Ireland before we left. I was not overly worried, but I was conscious of the fact that I had suffered a similar injury on the same knee three times already. And I was also aware that, even

Battling in the line-out with future Lions team-mate Geoff Parling during the 2013 Six Nations showdown with England at the Millennium Stadium.

Celebrating after our stunning 30-3 victory over England that secured the Six Nations title for Wales. It was one of the greatest moments in my career.

Walking through the assembled press, who had gathered for the announcement of the Lions squad at the Hilton Hotel in Syon Park. It was an early glimpse of the huge focus on the Lions.

Coach Warren Gatland and I pose with Bil, the tour mascot who had been discovered in Geneva airport.

There was a surprise party for me after the announcement of the Lions squad. My brother Ben and sister Holly stand on either side of me, while Rachel was taking the picture.

Landing in Hong Kong, we found a welcoming party to greet us as we prepared for the first leg of the tour.

Sadly, owing to a slight problem in my medial ligament, I wasn't able to train at the start of the tour, and was left sitting on the sidelines when I was desperate to get into the action.

Tempers flared in the stifling heat when Saracens team-mates Schalk Brits and Owen Farrell got in to a bust-up during the Lions' 59-8 victory over the Barbarians in the Hong Kong Stadium.

Neil Jenkins watches as Leigh Halfpenny lines up a conversion during the game against Western Force, which the Lions won 69-17, with Pence kicking 24 points.

At long last, I was a Lion. It was a great moment when I got to lead out the side for our game against the Queensland Reds.

Jonathan Davies and I go in to tackle Quade Cooper. It was my first game in seven weeks, so it took me a little while to get the rustiness out of my legs.

Indeed, I nearly scored a try, but I just couldn't force the ball down, and the television match official ruled against me. Happily, we still won 22-12 to make it three wins out of three.

Visiting the grave of Robert Seddon, the first Lions captain, with Andy Irvine and Manu Tuilagi. Maitland rugby club have kept the grave in immaculate condition.

The lads who were not involved in the game against the Combined Country side instead had a weights session.

Justin Tipuric finds himself surrounded during the Lions' comfortable 64-0 victory over the Combined Country side. There was always so much competition for Test spots in the back row.

Tackled by Matt Lucas during our hard-fought 47-17 victory over the Waratahs, but I felt I'd taken my game forward and was ready for the Test a week later.

I console Rob Kearney after a much-changed Lions side lost 14-12 to the Brumbies, but the next morning in training we were all determined to bounce back for the first Test.

My shirt for the first Test is embroidered with my name and Lions number. It's hard to describe just how much it meant to me, but as Sir Ian McGeechan told us: 'The jersey will come alive.' I was about to find out what he meant.

Leading out the Lions team for the first Test in Brisbane, we ran past the Tom Richards Cup. I was determined we would be taking it home with us at the end of the tour.

though I'd felt in good shape towards the end of the season, I had commented during the campaign that my body often starts to creak after 25 games in a season. Guess how many games I'd played before I went on the Lions tour? Yep, 25.

The injury was a medial ligament twinge. And I had suffered a grade two tear to that knee against France in Paris in 2011 (I could not carry on with that and left the field immediately), a grade one tweak against England at Twickenham in 2012 (I stayed on) and again against England in the Six Nations decider in Cardiff in 2013 (again, I stayed on but missed some Cardiff Blues games afterwards).

For about ten days afterwards, the injury was not getting any better and there was still some swelling around it, so they decided to give me a cortisone injection. I had to rest afterwards, that meant I was going to miss the Barbarians match. I had originally been picked to play in that and had even phoned home to tell my parents that I was going to make my Lions debut. I had also arranged with our operations director, Guy Richardson, to share a room with Dan Lydiate that week. Guy had spoken to me while we were training in Ireland and said that, as captain, if I ever wanted to have a single room or share with someone specifically then I should speak to him. And I do like to share a room with my blindside flanker (it helps that Dan is a great mate as well, of course) before a game, and that's exactly what I requested for this game.

The option of having a single room as captain is interesting. When I was first made Wales skipper in 2011, I was given a single room and I hated it. I made sure I always shared after that, but on this tour on a couple of occasions I did ask Guy if I could have some time alone. The first time was for two days in Newcastle, where we played the Combined New South Wales and Queensland Country team (I didn't play), and again for a couple of days in the build-up to the New South Wales Waratahs match in Sydney. I just found it good to have some time and space to myself and to be able to talk to my family freely on Skype or whatever.

Because I had had an injection, I knew there was some concern about my injury, and that's why I emailed my parents and Rachel immediately to tell them not to worry about it. I also think that's why the great James Robson might have been put up to speak about it. There was a lot of media concern and debate about the situation, and he was asked whether I was a doubt for the second match of the tour against Western Force in Perth: 'It depends where the boss wants to pick him,' he said. 'He had five days graduated return to play. You inject, you rest and then you give a graduated return to stress the injury, so he is in that progression. He has been doing training. He has not just been sitting around. It depends on the definition of training, for us it is rehabilitation training as opposed to rugby training.

'Sam is doing really well, and indeed he could have played against the Barbarians. The trouble was that he has had a previous injury to his leg there, so with anyone carrying or having had previous injuries we are always ultra-cautious. He has not got a privileged position because he is captain – we would have made the decision on anybody in that position. Last week, he just got a knock in training which seemed relatively innocuous. With the flight and stiffening up a little – despite the fact that we were lucky to fly business class, it is not the same as lying in your own bed – he just felt his knee a little bit. He didn't pull out of training at all, we pulled him out and advised Warren that we would rather give him a few days extra.

'My colleague Eanna Falvey thought it would be beneficial just to put a tiny bit of steroid around the area because that can help with the discomfort – and Sam has had enormous benefit from that. Given that he didn't play here, he should be available for the next game. It is a mild tweak of literally a few fibres of his ligament and possibly his muscle. It is not a dramatic injury.'

I was still gutted not to be playing, though. I can remember going back to the room to tell Dan, and he was gutted, too. We had always said since about 2010: 'How good would it be to play for the Lions together?' You just never know what is going to happen. It might have been that we never did start for the Lions. Of course, we did in the end, but at the time we didn't know. Despite it meaning that I missed the first match of the tour, I was glad that they decided to give me a cortisone injection. If they hadn't done so, I could easily have gone into the Barbarians game and not been right physically or mentally. It sorted the problem properly.

So Justin Tipuric took my place, which meant that there were still nine Welshmen (Alex Cuthbert, Jon Davies, Jamie

Roberts, Mike Phillips, Richard Hibbard, Adam Jones, Dan, Justin and Toby Faletau) in the side to take on the Barbarians. It had been obvious that the team for this match would consist mainly of those players who had been able to train at the camps in Cardiff and Ireland, rather than those who had been unable to join us until later on.

Paul O'Connell was appointed captain in my place and, in temperatures nearing 90°F and humidity levels approaching 90 per cent, Stuart Hogg was at full-back with Sean Maitland on the wing, Owen Farrell started at fly-half outside Mike, Mako Vunipola was alongside Richard and the Bomb (Adam) in the front row, and Richie Gray was in the second row with Paul.

The Barbarians were captained by Italy's Sergio Parisse and included three uncapped players – Ulster's Jared Payne at full-back, Wasps centre Elliot Daly and his team-mate, Sam Jones, at openside flanker. There were plenty of familiar faces for me: Dai Young, who was once my coach at Cardiff and, of course, three times a Lions tourist as a player, was their coach, and a former colleague at the Blues, Casey Laulala (now at Munster) was also playing in the centre. Wales prop Paul James started, and both James Hook and Duncan Jones were on the bench.

On the Thursday before this match, Andy Farrell showed us why he is so highly rated as a coach. At a team meeting he spoke with real passion about how we had to get our defensive mind-set right from the very start of the tour. The way he spoke and the language he used was seriously uplifting for all the boys. We were all bouncing after he spoke. I think every-one in the room could have gone out and played a game there and then, such was the impact of his words. It left me think-ing how much I would have liked to have played alongside him in his playing days. He must have been one tough cookie. After he had spoken, Warren looked to me to ask if I wanted to add anything. There was no way of following that, and no need. Andy had been awesome.

I got on really well with Graham Rowntree, or Wig as every-one calls him, on this tour as well. I thought he was a brilliant forwards coach. You could sense from the very start how desperate he was to win the series. And I liked what he said to me when I had dinner with the coaches before the team announcement in Syon Park. 'It's not what you say,' he said. 'It's what you do.'

And he said something similar to the press before the match against the New South Wales Waratahs later in the tour: 'He is a doer, and a lot of guys are following his lead in terms of his attitude to training, his diligence,' he said. I liked that. I think Warren may have had a word with him about what I was like as a captain, but I really appreciated those words. In fact, he seemed to me to be very like Warren in character.

When I was eventually picked for the first Test, Wig came up to me and said: 'Just become the best seven that's ever worn a Lions shirt,' and tapped me on the back. Those words stayed with me right up until kick off.

We beat the Barbarians 59-8, with tries from O'Connell, Phillips (2), Davies, Cuthbert (2), Lydiate and replacement

Alun-Wyn Jones. Owen Farrell kicked three penalties and three conversions, while replacement Jon Sexton also kicked two conversions.

What to make of it? I thought we were pretty good overall. The Barbarians obviously lacked preparation time, and we did not have to do a great deal of defending (conceding a try was still frowned upon, mind), but there were some really encouraging signs in attack. As Warren Gatland mentioned afterwards, there had been poor starts to the past two Lions tours in 2005 and 2009, so this was clearly a step up from that. Mike Phillips had an exceptional game, although he did get a bang on the knee that was to trouble him for the rest of the tour, and I thought all the back row were excellent. Paulie was outstanding and Mako made a fine first impression on tour, as did Jon Davies and Stuart Hogg. Furthermore, the conditions were horrendous, with the heat and humidity meaning there had to be frequent drinks breaks, and as a result the ball was like a bar of soap at times.

Despite the comprehensive nature of our win, much of the media attention focused on an incident involving Owen Farrell when he was holding his Saracens team-mate Schalk Brits at a ruck and Brits lost patience and punched him. Owen then retaliated. Brits was given a yellow card, but Warren made the point afterwards that we had to be careful about our discipline.

'It's pretty hard sometimes not to react when someone lands a punch square on your jaw,' he said. 'But we have to keep our discipline – that is hugely important to us on this tour.

Sometimes you have to take one for the team, by not retaliating when you get whacked, because the consequences of that retaliation can be reasonably severe as well. That is something we will stress to the players in the next couple of weeks. We might find ourselves in that situation in Australia and we have to make sure we don't react to that.'

There seemed to be quite a bit of negativity surrounding this game, with many pundits and commentators saying that the game was all about money and that we should have gone straight to Australia and prepared there. However, that was not the feeling from inside the camp that is for sure.

'We're going to get a benefit out of training, playing in those conditions,' Warren said. 'I'm looking at it as a positive. It's almost the same benefit as training at altitude. We definitely feel like the tour's started. The tour starts when you get on the plane and leave Britain and Ireland, but we are aware that the microscope is going to be on us a heck of a lot more than it is at the moment.'

Warren also made a point about drinking. Immediately after the match had finished, he had asked me, Paulie and Brian O'Driscoll what we thought should happen regarding drinking that night, and we gave our views. I think a few of the party were hoping to go out, but then Warren announced: 'Boys, I've had a chat with a few of the lads and we are not drinking tonight. We are going to Australia to do a job, so recover properly.'

It was time to fly to Perth, but there was a small problem. We knew beforehand that there would be only 36 business-class seats available, meaning one player would have to miss out. I had said to Andy Irvine and Guy Richardson that I would take the hit and go into economy class. But then my injury changed all that. As the team bus was leaving our Hong Kong hotel for the airport, Guy stood up and announced that I would not be flying in economy class, because the medical staff felt that it would be better for me to able to stretch out my leg in business class.

He told us that once we got to the airport, he would announce who that unlucky player was going to be, adding that it would not be anyone involved in the 23-man squad for the Western Force match in Perth or anyone who was carrying an injury. When it came to announcing who it was, it was hilarious. Guy really drew it out so that there was a lot of suspense. He kept whittling it down. He explained that Warren had said he was going to pick Jon Davies, but he is over 6ft tall and a centre, so he was out of the running. He said that this person had to be under 6ft. The net was closing. Then he concluded: 'And Warren said: "As an ex-hooker myself..."' At that moment, you could hear the swearing coming from the back of the bus as Richard Hibbard realised it was going to be him.

There was much cheering and abuse, and the boys were rubbing and slapping Hibbs's head. He is a great guy who is always dishing out the banter, so quite a few of the boys saw it as a chance to hurl a bit back at him! I don't think Hibbs was talking to me at this point. The ticket he was given had my name on it, and I had his.

There was more to this story, though. In one of the later

fines meetings, if you rolled a four on the dice, you could pick someone else to do your forfeit for you. So sure enough, Hibbs rolled a four. I thought he might pick me, but it wasn't me who had made the decision to move him. Instead, he turned straight to Gats and chose him!

Nobody could believe it. Gats looked astonished, that is for certain. It was a seriously brave move by Hibbs. Or stupid, if you wanted to look at it another way. That's because the forfeit on that occasion was you had to find your own way home from training, and poor Gats can hardly walk more than a few yards because of the nasty accident he suffered back home in New Zealand in the summer of 2012, when he fell and broke both his heels.

As it ended up, there were three of us who had to make our own way back to the team hotel after the captain's run (the light training session the day before a game) before the match against the New South Wales Waratahs in Sydney, the fifth fixture of the tour. I had been fined for wearing black shoes when I was meant to wear brown. Graham Rowntree was also fined, so it was Gats, Wig and myself who each had to thumb a lift back, because that was all we could do. We were not allowed to have any money or our mobile phone with us, and taxis were a big no-no! Luckily for me, it was a press day and I chanced upon the BBC Wales crew, including Ross Harries and Gareth Charles. So I asked them for a lift in their minibus and they duly obliged. They got to film it and take a few photos – and I promised them a feature after the tour – so everyone was happy.

I think Gats managed to get a lift with an Irish journalist. As for Wig, he got caught out. Andy Farrell phoned him and asked him what he was doing, but just by answering the call, he had handed himself in because he was supposed to be without his phone. The fine was duly doubled.

So we went on to Perth for a game against the Western Force. As soon as we arrived there, at the instigation of our Australian strength and conditioning coach, Adam Beard, we immediately hit the beach, even if it was only to have a swim in the sea and get rid of any stiffness. What we didn't realise was that there would be lots of photos taken of us as we emerged from the water. One of the daily papers back home printed a huge photo of me coming out of the water and compared me with Daniel Craig, when he was in his swimming trunks for a scene in the James Bond film *Casino Royale*. No surprise, then, that my room-mate on this leg of the trip, Tommy Bowe, was soon calling me James Bond and that I was hearing '007' mentioned a few times at training!

I took it in good heart, of course, but I have to say that that is not my style at all. I don't really like having photos taken with my top off. I made a mental note to wear a T-shirt the next time we had a beach recovery session. One of those photos from the beach was then used alongside one of David Beckham to illustrate an article about professional sportsmen shaving their chests. I only know that because someone tweeted that article. And although it was quite nice to be placed alongside David Beckham, I have to be honest and say that this was exactly the sort of publicity I don't like. I'll go further and say I hate that type of thing.

Having said that, it did allow me to have a bit of fun with Rachel. I said to her one day: 'You do know that I am in the same league as Daniel Craig and David Beckham now, don't you?' I was just pretending to be arrogant when she knows that I am anything but that. But when she finished her accountancy exams while I was out in Australia, I thought I would send her a card via Moonpig, which is a tool for sending personalised cards online. It was a picture of me with my top off on the beach, and inside it said: 'Well done on your exams ... 007' I think she liked it. She put it on Twitter anyway!

When we got to the match against the Force, they decided to field a second-string side against us because they had a Super Rugby fixture against the New South Wales Waratahs a few days later. They did, though, include a former Cardiff Blues' team-mate of mine, Sam Norton-Knight, at fly-half. If I'm honest, I cannot blame the Force for putting out a weakened side with a big game coming later in the week. To play two games in a week is very tough. I had already heard that the Queensland Reds would put out a stronger side in our next game, so I wasn't too worried. At least it gave us the opportunity to practise moves and get used to each other. So in hindsight I think it worked out well.

As for us, Warren picked a completely different starting line-up from the one that had beaten the Barbarians. It didn't include me, because it was felt that it was still too early after my injection, and Gats wanted me to play against the Queensland Reds at the weekend. The team for the Western Force match included eight Irishmen (Tommy Bowe, captain Brian O'Driscoll, Jon Sexton, Conor Murray, Cian Healy, Rory Best, Jamie Heaslip and Sean O'Brien), four Welshmen (Leigh Halfpenny, George North, Alun-Wyn Jones and Ian Evans) and three English players, all from Leicester (Manu Tuilagi, Dan Cole and Tom Croft). Four of those who started against the Barbarians were picked as replacements: Mako Vunipola, Toby Faletau, Owen Farrell and Sean Maitland.

We won this match 69-17, with nine tries and 24 points from Leigh's boot, taking his kicks from everywhere and not missing one. Brian scored two tries and there was one each for Jon Sexton, Tom Croft, Jamie Heaslip, Mako Vunipola, Tommy Bowe, Owen Farrell and Geoff Parling.

It was another good performance, marred only by the ankle injury to Cian Healy that ended his tour, although there was also some concern over the sloppy defence that allowed the Force to score two tries. And, of course, there was the standard of the opposition. As Warren said: 'You always want to play against stronger sides. That is a concern for us at the moment. You need the intensity. If we are not getting it from games like tonight, then we'll have to look at doing it ourselves – playing with a bit more intensity in training. It was a good workout, though, especially for those just starting the tour. The challenge for us coaches is who the hell are we going to pick for that first Test? At the moment, there is so much competition for places and that's good for us.'

Before this match there had been an important announcement. The 'Bobby Cup' was going to take place. Bobby is the

England conditioning coach Paul Stridgeon. He was once a wrestler and he is one of the funniest guys I have ever met. The day before the Western Force game he said to us: 'I know there have been a lot of rumours and whispering, but I can now reveal that the Bobby Cup is going ahead.' I'd heard about this before from the guys who had been on the 2009 tour, when he had done the same thing. They had talked about how funny it was, but I think he wanted to make sure it was OK with this group of coaches before he said he wanted to do it again.

The idea behind it was this: whenever we won two games in a row, it was time to award the Bobby Cup. It's not given for anything in particular, just to the person that Bobby believes has contributed something special to the tour, either on or off the field. As part of the ceremony, Bobby basically does a ten-minute comedy sketch into which he puts an awful lot of time and effort (apparently, he once spent three hours trying to find one small piece of video footage). For example, he might do a 'through the keyhole' feature on someone's room, or he would show clips that have the boys rolling with laughter.

For this first one, where Mako Vunipola won the cup for his early tour performances, Bobby had some great clips of Andy Farrell scrapping when he was playing and some funny pictures of Graham Rowntree doing interviews. They were all absolutely hilarious, and Bobby was awesome in keeping the boys' morale up throughout the tour. Every day he was full of energy and full of the whole Lions concept. He would always be down at the front of the bus, beeping the horn at the Lions fans who were walking the streets in their red shirts. It was a huge red and unmistakably Lions-branded bus, so when the fans saw us beeping and waving they would go nuts. Bobby was brilliant. Getting to know him was definitely a highlight of the tour.

4

A Lion at Last

My wait was finally over when I got to pull on the British and Irish Lions shirt against Queensland Reds. Two games had passed on the tour already and I hadn't appeared because of that minor knee injury. And that was tough. I think by this stage only Rob Kearney, Gethin Jenkins and I from the original tour party had not played a game.

However much you say that you are not, you do feel out of the loop slightly. Everyone was on this Lions tour to play, and we were all desperate for our first involvement on the pitch. But I also thought I needed only one game to prove myself for Test selection, so I didn't panic about missing the first two games. Coming off the back of a tough domestic and international season, I reckoned it might have been a good thing in a way, as I really wanted to stay fit from start to finish in an end-of-season tour. By reducing my game time early on, I believed that, from a selfish point of view, this might actually be better for my chances of finishing the tour. Not that I could really say that sort of thing publicly at the time.

'This Lions experience has felt special, even though I haven't been playing,' I said. 'I certainly haven't felt left out of things. But I've been thinking about this match for two or three weeks now, and I can't wait to get on the pitch and put in a decent display.'

It must have been worse for Rob, because he wasn't even involved in this match either. He had had a hamstring injury and did not appear until he came off the bench in the fifth game of the tour, against the New South Wales Waratahs. As for Gethin, he was picked for this match against the Queensland Reds, but then unfortunately had to pull out the day before. He was still struggling with a calf injury that he had picked up when coming on for Toulon in the Heineken Cup final against Clermont Auvergne in Dublin. He had a scan and, on the morning of the Queensland Reds game, it was announced that, sadly, he was returning home.

On the same day, Alex Corbisiero arrived from England's tour of Argentina, having taken flights from Salta in Argentina to Buenos Aires, to Santiago in Chile, then to Auckland, next to Sydney and then finally to Brisbane where he met up with us before this match at the Suncorp Stadium, which was going to be the venue for the first Test two weeks later.

Despite what I'd said, and the way I had rationalised it to myself, I'd found it especially hard missing the first match against the Barbarians in Hong Kong. Those of us not involved in the match-day 23 got to the ground first and we went into the changing rooms to see them decked out in Lions flags and the jerseys carefully laid out, with the players' names and their cap numbers on them. It was gutting to see that and not to be involved. I just so wanted to call myself a Lion, and I couldn't do that until I had played. As I've said, I shared a room with Dan Lydiate, who obviously played in that match, and it was such a long week for me. I kept going back to the room and seeing his Lions jerseys draped over the bath.

Every time I went to the toilet I would see them, and every time I looked at them they would make me feel so jealous! I don't mind admitting that. Dan is one of my best mates so I was delighted for him, but there was also a part of me that was feeling very envious. It was even worse when Dan came back to the room after the match. I kept asking him: 'What is it like?'

'What?' he replied.

'How does it feel to be a Lion?' I said.

I suppose it was also a good measure of how excited and motivated I was by the time it came to playing against the Queensland Reds. The side to face the Reds reflected the fact that Warren Gatland had always said that he would try to make sure that every member of the squad would start at least one of the first three matches.

Ben and Tom Youngs became the first brothers to start together for the Lions for 20 years, and there were starts for Matt Stevens and Geoff Parling, while Mako Vunipola was drafted in late for Gethin to start his second match in three. Manu Tuilagi and Tommy Bowe were the only two survivors from that starting line-up against the Western Force. There were also starts for two backs in positions that were not necessarily their first choices: Jon Davies at inside-centre and

Tommy on the left wing. And I was part of an all-Welsh back row alongside Dan and Toby Faletau. Finally, I was to get to play alongside Dan in a Lions shirt after all. But, with the likes of Jamie Heaslip, Sean O'Brien and Justin Tipuric already having put in strong performances, there was a lot of talk about the battle for the Test spots in the back row.

As the press was debating the issue, I thought the best thing to do was to deal with it head-on, so I said: 'I always thought the back row would be one of the strongest positions. It's always going to be a tough ask to play there for the Lions. I've definitely got to fight as hard as anyone in the squad. I was honest with Warren Gatland and told him that what I don't like about captaincy is knowing you've got a starting place. You want to have butterflies like everyone else. I like those feelings. They are what drive you in training to be a better player.'

We knew that this was going to be a tough match. This was definitely going to be a step up from the previous two games in terms of intensity (there was going to be a 50,000 crowd) and quality of opposition. Even if they were missing seven members of the Australian squad at the time, the Reds were still including nine capped Wallabies, including fly-half Quade Cooper, who we knew would pose a very different attacking threat from anything we had faced before on tour. But we knew that would be good. There was no way we wanted to go into the first Test with our defence undercooked, and that had been a valid concern after the first two matches.

I was pretty bullish in the pre-match press conference,

saying that we should aim to go through the whole tour undefeated. 'It might sound a bit disrespectful saying we can go through undefeated, but I remember an old PE teacher [Gwyn Morris at Whitchurch High School in Cardiff] telling me that if you aim high then, even if you fall short, you will achieve more than you thought possible. You've got to aim for the stars. It's not going to be easy by any means, but it's a goal and we've got to aim for it.'

Of course, no Lions team had won every game for well over a century, although the 1974 squad in South Africa had managed 21 wins and a draw. I knew that, but I also knew that we had made some sort of statement by scoring 17 tries and 128 points in the first two matches.

The good news was that my knee was fine. I had trained fully for the first time on the Wednesday before the game and there were no problems at all with it. As I've said already, all I had done was tweak a few fibres in my medial ligament. There were certainly no alarm bells as to how serious it was. I couldn't even remember a specific incident when it happened, so it can't have been too bad. I felt ready for action.

When we went into the changing rooms at the Suncorp Stadium, the plaque was there above my spot. It was real now: I was going to be a Lion. On the grey background was the British and Irish Lions badge and underneath was written: 'Sam Warburton. 800.' I was the 800th player to represent the Lions. It was certainly a proud moment for me, and it seemed auspicious that I'd got that number.

When I ran out on to the pitch, the atmosphere was like

that of an international. The crowd was predominantly Australian, as most Lions fans had not yet come out by this stage, and they made a lot of noise! But I always love that; away crowds never put me off, because it is always a great feeling when you can silence them.

It merely added to what was certainly a tough match in which to make my first appearance. We won 22-12, but the Reds really gave us a hard time, especially in the first 20 minutes. That period was incredibly quick. It was so quick, in fact, it was just like Wales's first Test against Australia at the same ground on the summer tour in 2012, which was similarly intense. But unlike that Test, which Wales lost 27-19, at least the Lions won this match.

We never panicked. That was the key. It was a really good hit-out for us, because we were put under significant pressure in defence, which we hadn't experienced in the games before. It was good that we went through that then, rather than in the first Test. And it was great to see the way the players responded under pressure. I never felt at any stage that we lost control. We knew we had to weather that initial storm, gain some territory and get some points on the board. The Reds had some great support and were clearly really up for the game, and I thought we dealt with that quite well.

There was no doubt it was a lively opening. Twice in the first three minutes, the Reds could have scored through chip-and-chase efforts down the left. And they came even closer when only some excellent defence (a good tackle by Stuart Hogg) stopped centre Ben Tapuai and then wing Rod Davies from scoring. We responded as Alex Cuthbert very nearly scored after a brilliant break from deep by Tommy Bowe. But their winger Luke Morahan made a good tackle to stop Cuthie and it was not a try, even though the television official had a look at it.

We were about to see a lot more of Morahan, as he also denied Owen Farrell a try by knocking the ball out of his hands, and then he scored a stunning try of his own. He caught a kick near his own 22-metre line and beat four defenders before chipping over Stuart Hogg to collect and score under the posts. Yes, I was one of those defenders, but Morahan was flying and I was off balance as I covered back. I don't think it was an exaggeration to say that it was one of the great tries scored in Lions history. It was that good.

On a personal level, I thought this match was a good start for me. There was room for improvement for sure – there always is – but I hadn't played for seven weeks. I'm like most other players in that it takes me time to get back up to speed in a match situation. It was about getting my timing back at the breakdown and getting some match fitness in as well. I thought I did that reasonably well, especially in gaining a couple of good turnovers.

It would have been nice to have scored in that match, though. And I very nearly did late in the first half as I got over the line in a close call that needed referral to the television match official. We were 13-7 up by this stage, after Ben Youngs (who had a really good game) had scored for us when there was some confusion at the back of a Reds scrummage and No 8 Jake Schatz lost control of the ball for Ben to pounce. Owen was on good form with the boot, and was to finish with a 100 per cent record and 17 points in the match.

What happened with my effort was that I took the ball from George North, who had come on as a replacement at centre instead of the injured Manu Tuilagi (shoulder), and it reminded me of the try I scored against Fiji in the 2011 World Cup. But here their winger came from nowhere and it spooked me a bit. I thought I was going to have a clear run. Watching the video afterwards, I realised I should have transferred the ball into my left hand and used my right hand to fend him off, but I cut back inside instead. I definitely got the ball over the line, but there was a hand underneath it – and maybe Quade Cooper's leg as well – and I remember trying to twist the ball left and right so that it might make some contact with the grass.

I wasn't sure whether I had touched it down or not. The boys were asking me and I was saying: 'It's fifty-fifty, I'm just not sure.' Mind you, it was pretty hard work keeping up with George – the whole move was probably about 80m after beginning to support the break – so from my point of view the longer the television match official took the better so I could recover. And of course it would have been superb to have scored a try for the Lions – every player dreams of that – but it was not to be. It had been an incredible break from George, who had collected the ball inside our own 22, and as I was tracking back I had met him at our ten-metre line, before turning and sprinting to keep up with him.

We were 16-7 up at half time, and then 19-7 after another penalty from Owen with half an hour to go. But heavy rain had come down, making conditions difficult, so, with our scrummage dominant, we tried to keep things relatively tight. Their scrum-half Nick Frisby scored a try, though, to make it 19-12 and we were quite happy that Mike Harris, the man whose brilliant last-minute penalty had robbed Wales of victory over Australia in Melbourne in 2012, missed the conversion because the Reds still needed two scores to win with 15 minutes remaining. We coped with that last period reasonably well and Owen kicked another penalty with three minutes left so that we won 22-12.

As I said afterwards: 'It was great to get the win, it was a really tough one. We expected that all week. It was great for us – we knew the Reds in attack would offer a lot today and they made it tough for us.'

I also commented about my own performance and fitness: 'It's always a bonus to come through injury free. The medics did a great job over the last few weeks. My knee feels fantastic now and I have no problems with it. I haven't played for seven weeks, so I'm pleased I came through seventy-five minutes. It was good to get used to the tempo. It reminded me very much of the first Test we played out here with Wales last summer. We will benefit from it hugely. A lot of aspects of the game went very well for us.

'Wanting to go through unbeaten might come across as a bit arrogant to some people, but it's just a goal. It was a challenge put to me by tour manager Andy Irvine. Being very ambitious, I liked the sound of it. It's always going to be tough. I found that out the hard way, playing in Australia quite a few times with little success. We're extremely confident with the squad we've got here. There's just so much class and I think it's definitely achievable.'

The only downside for us was the broken hand that Tommy Bowe had suffered required surgery, which meant a call for Simon Zebo from Ireland's tour of North America. There was also a slight doubt about Jon Sexton, who had a tight hamstring, but I know that Warren Gatland was really pleased with the way things had gone.

'I'm very, very happy,' he said afterwards. 'This was exactly what we wanted. We would like a couple more lead-in games, and for the first two games to be a bit tougher than they were, but that's what happens on tour – you are not dealing with tough teams all the time. I thought the set-piece was where the game was won. If you look at the way the Reds played – tactically, maybe Australia will do the same thing – they kept the ball in the park and only had about four line-outs. It was like watching Wales play against other teams. I thought our scrum was excellent and the line-out very good defensively. There needs to be a huge amount of credit placed on that part of our game.'

All was good, then, as we moved up country to Newcastle to face the Combined Country team. I wasn't playing in that game – Justin Tipuric was at seven alongside Sean O'Brien and Jamie Heaslip in the back row – but there was a debut for the recently arrived Alex Corbisiero, and Ryan Grant, who had

come from Scotland's tour of South Africa, was on the bench.
Three players – Richie Gray, Alex Cuthbert and Stuart Hogg –
were starting their second games on the trot, while George
North had come off the bench early against the Reds. Brian
O'Driscoll was captain and joined in the centre by Jamie
Roberts for the first time since they had had such a successful
partnership on the 2009 Lions tour of South Africa.

For me the trip to Newcastle was poignant as I visited the
grave of Robert Seddon, the Lions' first captain to New
Zealand and Australia in 1888, who tragically drowned on the
River Hunter in a sculling accident. Seddon had recently been
given a Lions number (11) and here I was, the 32nd Lions
captain and number 800, visiting his grave.

I went to the cemetery at West Maitland with Manu Tuilagi,
as well as tour manager Andy Irvine, Lions chairman Gerald
Davies and our chief executive John Feehan. The grave there
has been looked after for the past 80 years by members of the
Maitland rugby club, which, apparently, is the second oldest in
Australia, having been founded in 1877. The grave is
absolutely immaculate and it was humbling to know that the
locals have kept it in such a wonderful condition in memory of
our first Lions captain. Also at the ceremony, where I laid a
wreath on Seddon's grave, were the president of the Australian
Rugby Union, David Crombie, the president of Maitland
Rugby Club, Dan Lewer, and the local MP, Tim Owen.

Apparently, Seddon had led the Lions to victory in their first
game against Otago in Dunedin in April 1888, and played in
21 rugby and 19 Victorian Rules matches (there were 54

matches in total on the tour!), before his tragic accident three days after a match against Sydney University. He was just 28, and was buried the next day in his red, white and blue hooped Lions jersey.

As players we are very aware of the history of the Lions, and having former players such as Andy and Gerald on tour with us helped that. When they spoke, we all realised that this tour was not just about the players that were there, it was about representing 125 years of Lions history. It made it even more special.

'This is where it all started one hundred and twenty-five years ago and we are all very grateful to have this opportunity to visit the grave of our first captain,' I said. 'I'm sure the next time the Lions come to Australia there will be other players who will visit him again. The grave is immaculate and looks like one of the best kept in the cemetery. As it belongs to the first Lions captain, it is very nice of them to do that.'

I was asked about the Australian Rules aspect of Seddon's tour, which I found amazing. 'I've got a godmother in Brisbane who is going to educate me in Aussie Rules and we're going to catch a game next time I'm there,' I said. 'But at the moment, I don't know much about it.'

I'd actually been to see my godmother, Jane, for a barbeque on our day off on the Sunday after the Queensland Reds game. It was great to see her, and we had a great time with plenty of food. I think I saw Dan Lydiate eat a record amount of prawns. He was starving, and must have eaten nearly 30 large prawns ... and that was just for starters!

A Lion at Last

Jane has a bullmastiff dog called Misty, whom we all loved, as my family are such dog lovers. It was great spending time with Misty, as she reminded me of my parents' dogs back home. Mentally, it was a great trip for me to escape from the rugby just for a day and to act normally as I would back home. Those quiet moments the day after a game are precious, and I made sure that I enjoyed them whenever I could, but it was never easy on such a high-profile and high-intensity trip. That short period when you've played one game and do not yet have to think about the next one are like gold dust. They are the only time you can really relax. My parents and Rachel (and Dan's fiancée, Nia) were to stay with Jane for the first Test in Brisbane and I saw her again then.

In an interview before he died Seddon had shocked the locals in Australia by saying he didn't think the Australian players were as tough as those he had played against in New Zealand, and perhaps inevitably I was asked about that. 'After the Queensland game last weekend, I can't agree with him there,' I said. 'It was one of the toughest games I've played in and exactly what we needed – it was a great game.'

We won the match against the Combined Country team comfortably, by 64-0. It made it four from four on the tour at that point, and you couldn't really complain about that. The Combined team had 12 players with Super Rugby experience in their squad, but they also had a builder, a plumber, a carpenter, an electrical engineer and a medical student in there, too. It was certainly unusual, and so I could see why some people were arguing that the games could have been more competitive, but they were still good run-outs in which we could work on moves and our work at the contact area. Even though we won 64-0, we still benefited in a number of ways from that match.

There were ten tries in all, two from George North, and one each for Alex Cuthbert, Conor Murray, Jon Davies, Stuart Hogg, Richard Hibbard, Brian O'Driscoll, Leigh Halfpenny and Sean O'Brien. Hoggy kicked four conversions and Leigh two. When Hoggy hit the post with the attempted conversion of his own try in the 12th minute, remarkably it was the first kick we had missed on tour in Australia. That's not to have a go at Hoggy, just to stress the brilliance of the kicking. Neil Jenkins, the kicking coach, was doing his job pretty well!

It was 38-0 at half time, and if we were honest, we got a little sloppy in the second half. But as Warren stressed: 'It was a lot of use. That team only had one training session together. There was some excellent stuff, and there was some average stuff as well. There were a few turnovers. There is great harmony within the squad. We are undefeated, so if we can win the next two games we will arrive in Brisbane undefeated. We will be in a good, positive frame of mind.'

The next game was against the New South Wales Waratahs in Sydney, and I was chosen to play my second game of the tour. It was an interesting selection. I had a funny feeling that the pack might be similar to the one Warren was thinking about for the first Test. It was Mako Vunipola, Tom Youngs, Adam Jones, Alun-Wyn Jones, Paul O'Connell, Tom Croft, Jamie Heaslip and myself. I didn't know that would be the case, of course – I was never on selection – but it was just the feeling I had. And it was not as if I could say as much publicly, not least because we all had to perform first.

'You always want game time and the more games I have the better I will play,' I said. 'You pick up a feel for the contact area and the speed of the game. I am looking forward to playing with Tom and Jamie. Everyone wants to impress, no matter what the game. We always put that pressure on ourselves, but nobody is reading too much into anything.'

Warren was certainly making sure that no one was complacent, especially those of us in the back row. 'We have far from made up our minds about the loose forwards,' he said. 'There are a huge amount of options and possible combinations. They are all fit and that will be a headache for us. We're still looking at combinations. These players have a great opportunity on Saturday. A good performance will go a long way, but the Test team won't be selected until after Tuesday.'

There was inevitably a question about my Test place. 'I think I've been one hundred per cent consistent from day one; it's about picking the best players,' Warren said. 'Sam's well aware of that. He had a good blowout last week against the Reds, he had a couple of good turnovers, so let's see what happens on Saturday rather than trying to create some controversy about potentially leaving one or two players out of the team.'

As it was, there was only one change from that pack for the first Test, with Alex Corbisiero being preferred to Mako Vunipola at loose-head prop.

In the backs, things were a little more complicated for this match. The good news was that both Jon Sexton and Owen Farrell were fit for selection after suffering minor injury worries. Jon started, with Owen on the bench. George North missed out, though, with a hamstring problem, as did Brian O'Driscoll who had done the splits at the end of the Combined Country match and had woken up the next day feeling some pain. Warren had spoken about managing Brian before the start of the tour, and making sure that he played only one game a week. Rob Kearney was picked for his first appearance of the tour, from among the replacements, after recovering from a hamstring injury. And his Irish colleague, Simon Zebo, was included in the starting team just two days after arriving to join us. With Manu Tuilagi still having a sore shoulder, it had also been decided to call England's Billy Twelvetrees from Argentina.

'We have a few knocks in the backs,' said Warren. 'We need to make sure we rest a few players, because the whole priority is making sure that we arrive in Brisbane next Saturday fresh and ready to go. The thinking with bringing Billy Twelvetrees in was that we need cover for the midfield. Brian is sore from the last game and Manu still has a sore shoulder. We wanted to bring Billy in to be available to play in the game on Tuesday [against the Brumbies].'

The Waratahs might have been without eight Wallaby squad members, but they were strengthened by the return of flanker Dave Dennis and centre Rob Horne, who had been released by coach Robbie Deans from the Australia squad, as well as fly-half Bernard Foley and replacement back Matt Lucas who'd been released from the Australia sevens squad.

We won the match 47-17, scoring five tries, and I thought we made a considerable statement ahead of the first Test in Brisbane. The Queensland game had been the toughest warm-up game, with its international intensity for the first half, but by the second half of that match we had taken more control of the game. So now, by this match against the Waratahs, we had experienced the speed of Super Rugby and adjusted to it well, and this wasn't as much of a shock to the system.

We were indebted to Leigh Halfpenny, who contributed 30 points, including two tries, as well as four conversions and four penalties. Owen Farrell kicked one conversion and there were also tries from Jon Sexton, Tom Croft and Jon Davies. There were fine individual performances from Mako Vunipola, Tom Croft, Alun-Wyn Jones, Paul O'Connell and Tom Youngs. And I thought I took my own game up a notch from the week before, as I always seem to do with more game time. I made 12 tackles. But all in all, it was a good team effort.

The only negative was the hamstring injury suffered by Jamie Roberts, which left us playing with 14 men for the last seven minutes of the match, and that injury was eventually to put him out of the first two Tests. Mind you, Jon Davies had a stormer of a match, and when Brian O'Driscoll came into the dressing room afterwards he immediately said: 'Man! How good was Jonathan Davies?' That is high praise.

But, still, after the match the decision was made to call up three extra backs. England's Christian Wade and Brad Barritt were summoned, and there was a shock call for my old team-mate Shane Williams, who was in Japan, and was added to the squad just as temporary cover. It was strange because it seemed that all the backs were going down injured, and I think Warren and the rest of the management were realising that the original selection of just 16 backs might not have been quite enough.

This was a very physical game, with quite a lot of stuff happening off the ball, something I spoke about to referee Jaco Peyper on a few occasions. As I mentioned earlier, it's when you have hot-headed, emotional conversations that referees tend not to listen, so you need to be quite measured in your approach, which was what I did here. You don't want to try to tell them how to referee a game – they know how to do it – it's just a matter of trying to make them aware of things that might be going on. They can't see everything, and against the Waratahs it was a competitive game and there was a lot going on, but I thought Jaco dealt with it very well.

I was, though, careful not to make too much fuss about this afterwards. 'The Waratahs were really tough and I don't think the score reflected the way they played, but we definitely stepped up and I knew we had to,' I said. 'I thought the forwards did a great job and the backs were very clinical, so I'm very pleased with the performance. From watching the Waratahs, we knew they were very similar to us and very direct.'

Warren did not want to create a stir either but, still, he made his point clearly enough. 'There were little shoulder charges

and guys being taken late,' he said. 'There was some provoca-
tion out there, but it is how you respond to that niggle and our
boys were magnificent. The big key in this game was keeping
our discipline. The nine and ten were being tackled off the
ball. It would have been easy enough for someone to be taken
late, lose their head and throw a punch and then be cited. We
felt there has been a little bit of off-the-ball stuff in the first
couple of games, but we said we were not going to bitch and
moan about it. We are not going to get involved in any accu-
sations against the opposition.'

We might have scored in the very first minute of the game,
but Simon Zebo unfortunately put a foot in touch after a great
run, but we had shown our attacking intent, and within six
minutes we were 10-0 up after a try from Jon Sexton, created
by Jon Davies, with Leigh Halfpenny kicking the conversion
and a penalty.

Jon Sexton in particular seemed to be being targeted and,
while he was down after being clattered by one of their forwards, the Waratahs scored a long-range try. But he was soon
back on his feet and helping in an excellent try from Leigh just
before half time. With three more kicks from Leigh it was
23-10 at the interval.

Just after half time, Leigh scored again, this time after good
work from Jamie Roberts and Jon Davies. And it was Jon who
set up Tom Croft's typical galloping try from out wide. He
showed some serious pace for a flanker! And then Jon himself
finished off proceedings with a try late on.

Another win and on the tour went. Although there was a

match on the Tuesday, against the Brumbies, the truth was that all eyes were turning to the first Test in Brisbane on the Saturday, and who might be fit. Jamie hadn't pulled a hamstring before, but it seemed pretty certain that was the injury he had, and George North was probably only about 50:50 at this stage for the Test with his own hamstring injury. Tommy Bowe, though, had had his operation on his hand and was out of his cast. Already it looked like he might be fit for the second Test.

Those playing against the Brumbies knew they were unlikely to start in the Test. That was why Christian Wade, Brad Barritt, Billy Twelvetrees and Shane Williams had been drafted in and why they were all picked to start against the Brumbies in Canberra, in a side captained by Rory Best. Rob Kearney was at full-back with Stuart Hogg again at fly-half outside Ben Youngs. Ryan Grant and Matt Stevens were the props, with Ian Evans and Richie Gray in the second row, and there was a back row of Sean O'Brien, Toby Faletau and Justin Tipuric.

I know there was some criticism of Shane being called up, but I personally thought it was a great call in the circumstances. He has got that aura about him and players want to play alongside him. For someone like Christian Wade to do that it was a pretty special moment.

But, of course, things were not easy from a continuity point of view in terms of training and preparation, with all these new players having to learn the patterns and calls so quickly. That was always going to be a pretty tough ask. So it was perhaps not a huge surprise that we lost the match 14-12. It was a horrible, cold evening. And there had even been snow in the area, which made some contrast with how we'd started the tour in the heat of Hong Kong. But we never really got going, struggling badly up front where the line-outs did not go well and we were put under enormous pressure at every contact situation.

There was only one try on the evening, and that was scored by the Brumbies, when Andrew Smith made a good run for Tevita Kuridrani to score. We hit the posts with two penalties, which obviously might have made a difference, but the Brumbies probably deserved to win in the end, even if it was not a great game and they did not really try to play much rugby. But they were well drilled and played well enough. They were very direct and hard off the line, winning the collisions and making it very hard for us to get our game going. They won the battle of the gain-line and slowed our ball down.

I thought Rory Best was admirably honest in his assessment as captain afterwards. 'We got physically beaten up up-front, we got a bit nervy and they were hungrier than us right across the board,' he said. 'The forwards will stand up and take a lot of the heat and deservedly so. We just didn't turn up. Right from the start, they wanted it more. We let our standards slip and it's up to the twenty-three this weekend to raise them again.'

I'd said previously that I was looking for an unbeaten tour, as we all were as players, but I also think we were realistic to know that there might be disappointments along the way. The key was always how we responded to them and whether we learnt from them. You could see that the boys were not hit too badly by the loss immediately afterwards on Wednesday morning when there was plenty of laughter and banter. We had five players in the backline playing for the first time, so I thought that for a scratch team we did the best we could, which is all you can ask. The result didn't go our way, but it didn't knock our confidence at all.

If we needed any perspective, we had been provided with it on the day before the game when I had led a delegation to the Australian War Memorial in Canberra. It is a magnificent building with a really impressive museum underneath. I found the whole trip fascinating, and it was good to widen my history knowledge as well as pay our respects. I went with Richie Gray, Tom Croft and Rory Best, along with Andy Irvine, and we took part in a moving ceremony there. We all laid poppies on the monument and I also laid a wreath, as we remembered the thousands of Australian soldiers who gave their lives in the two world wars.

We also remembered some Lions who had served with such distinction in the First World War. First there was Major Blair Swannell, who won seven Test caps for the Lions in Australia in 1899 and then in New Zealand in 1904, but who did not return home, settling in Sydney before winning one cap for Australia in 1905. He was killed in action at Anzac Cove on the first day of the Gallipoli Campaign in 1915. Another Lions tourist who decided to stay on in Australia, John Leaper Fisher, also served in Gallipoli.

Tom Richards was another who saw action in Gallipoli and went on to win the Military Cross in 1917. It was the trophy named after him that we were playing for on this tour, just as the Lions and Australia had first done in 2001. Richards played for Australia in matches against Wales and England in 1908-09 and he had also been a member of the Australian team that won a gold medal at the London Olympic Games in 1908. He sailed to South Africa during the Lions tour there in 1910 and was asked to play when injuries struck. He played two Tests, including the final one when the Lions won 8-3.

And it was Test matches to which we were now turning our attention in Australia. They were always what really mattered. If we could win the Test series, with all due respect nobody would ever really remember a midweek defeat against the Brumbies.

It was time to think about the first of those Tests in Brisbane.

5

First Test, Last Kick

It was an anxious time. Selection for the first Test was what everyone had been waiting for. It was what everyone had come to Australia for, after all. I'll let you into a little secret and say that I knew that I was playing before the others, because Warren Gatland had asked me on the Monday to go with him to meet the referee Chris Pollock on the Wednesday. It was a pretty big clue that I was in.

On the Thursday the team was announced publicly (with the players having been told on the Wednesday) and it was the second largest press conference I have been in. Only the conference before the World Cup semi-final against France in 2011 comes close. I had had a sense all tour that the press were waiting for me to show nerves or provide some evidence that I was feeling the pressure. At this point I honestly wasn't. I don't feel nerves until match day. So when a journalist asked me how I felt to be leading the Lions in a Test at the young age of 24 and how I would cope with all the responsibilities of being captain, I played the whole situation down and just replied: 'Happy days!'

I suppose the one surprise to those outside the squad was the inclusion of Alex Corbisiero at loose-head prop. He had not been an original selection for the tour and had played just one full game, against the Combined Country team. He had also not previously played on tour alongside his Test hooker Tom Youngs. But I think Warren had looked at the weather forecast, which suggested showers were possible, so he wanted Corbs' extra technical expertise at the scrummage, thinking that Mako Vunipola could come off the bench later and make a really powerful impact in the loose.

'I've no doubt that [Australia coach] Robbie Deans has looked at Mako technically at scrum time,' said Warren. 'Mako coming off the bench will give us a huge amount of impetus and that's a big strength of his game. Technically, Alex is probably a little bit sounder and potentially we feel we might have a little bit of an edge at scrum time, although it will be tough contest.'

I remember Graham Rowntree saying to me when we spoke at Syon Park that Mako could have a real impact off the bench, so I was thinking then that he might be in with a shout of a Test spot on the bench. However, the tour unfolded for the loose-head props rather differently from how anyone would have expected, and Mako had played so well that I thought he would start, mainly because he had been on tour for longer than Corbs and knew the calls and the patterns better. That is not to be disrespectful to Corbs, who is a superb player, as he was to show in this series.

Otherwise it was the same pack that had started against the

New South Wales Waratahs. In fact, 11 of the team from that game were selected, with Alex Cuthbert, George North and Brian O'Driscoll coming in for Sean Maitland, Simon Zebo and the injured Jamie Roberts. It meant Jon Davies had to play in his less accustomed position of inside centre and in a partnership with Brian that had only had 23 minutes together in the match against the Combined Country team. Jon had been under pressure, in terms of selection issues for the Waratahs match, and he had been quite outstanding, so we knew they would work well together despite this lack of time on the pitch.

The overall message seemed to be that the match against the Waratahs had settled a lot of selection issues, and players were being rewarded for their performances then. There were obviously a lot of disappointed players, just as you would expect, but Andy Irvine spoke to us and used the example of the last tour in 2009 to South Africa, where there had been so many changes to the Test side between the first Test and the third Test.

As I said earlier, I was not involved in selection at all, but while we were waiting to see Chris Pollock before this match I did say to Gats: 'I'd love to be a fly on the wall for one of your selection meetings.'

He replied: 'You can come and sit in on the next one, if you want.' I remember thinking how that would be awesome, though I wouldn't have wanted to contribute because that would not have been my place, but it would have been a fascinating insight. Then, after giving it some more thought, I realised that it would not be such a good idea. Thinking like a fan, it would be great to be in there, but not as a player. It would not be right that I knew what certain coaches thought of certain players. As I said earlier, I've always wanted just to be one of the boys and not be given preferential treatment and assume I will be selected, even if I am captain. If my team-mates knew that I had been sitting in on a selection meeting, I don't think it would have gone down too well.

There were eight of the Wales team involved (Leigh Half-penny, Alex Cuthbert, Jon Davies, George North, Mike Phillips, Adam Jones, Alun-Wyn Jones and myself) and seven players who had played in Lions Tests before – Brian O'Driscoll, Phillsy, Adam, Alun-Wyn, Paul O'Connell, Tom Croft and Jamie Heaslip. I had Brian and Paulie alongside me as former Lions tour captains and I think that about half the pack had been captains of their countries. There was certainly no lack of experience. Ben Youngs was the only player who had started against the Brumbies and was now in the Test 23, and he was picked on the bench ahead of Conor Murray. Alongside him were Richard Hibbard, Mako Vunipola, Dan Cole, Geoff Parling, Dan Lydiate, Owen Farrell and Sean Maitland.

The back row was clearly a position of strength and one area where selection had been particularly difficult. I thought all along that we had seven players there who could all start a Test and you'd be happy. That's how competitive it was, but the seven of us are very different players and all seven had done well and played their parts up until then. In the end, the selectors went for me, Tom Croft and Jamie Heaslip, with Dan as the only cover on the bench. That also might have surprised some people, because Dan might not be seen as the sort of player you would normally expect to see coming off the bench in the back row. But Warren had a plan, and that was to tighten things up later on rather than open them up.

I was looking forward to playing alongside Tom and Jamie. Crofty had already shown on the tour what he could do in areas like re-starts and the line-out, while he was also a real threat with ball in hand, as was Jamie, who had also shown some great work on the floor as well. Crofty is one of the best line-out forwards I have ever seen. In the air, his hands and athleticism are superb. I remember saying to Graham Rowntree that I had been watching the video analysis and I was hugely impressed by Crofty's footwork going into certain jumps, and how consistent he was in doing that.

I actually noticed how technically advanced all the Leicester boys were when it came to line-out time. They were so specific about every single movement – from Geoff Parling and Crofty with their jumps to Dan Cole with his lifting. But in praising Crofty that is in no way denigrating Dan. I honestly thought it was always going to be a 50:50 call between the two. The selection for the Waratahs match had suggested it was going to be Crofty, but I also knew Warren had always said that to beat Australia you have to be really physical. And if that was the game plan, then it would better suit Dan.

Having said all this, I know that Dan was genuinely pleased to be picked on the bench. I think he thought that he would be starting or not be involved at all. When he heard Crofty was starting, he thought that was it for him and that Sean O'Brien would be on the bench, so he was delighted. But I thought the starting balance was good with Crofty and Jamie, and I had really enjoyed playing with the pair of them against the Waratahs. It might have been a little bit of a case of trying to figure out things on the go, but that is always what Lions tours are about – learning to play with different players and picking up new things.

As for Australia, they had picked three new caps in flanker Ben Mowen, inside centre Christian Lealiifano and wing Israel Folau. Understandably, there was a lot of interest in Folau, who was in his first season of professional rugby union, having already played for Australia at rugby league and also the Australian Football League (AFL). We were well aware what a quality player and a supreme athlete Folau is, but he had been playing at full-back for the New South Wales Waratahs and he was now on the wing. It is not the easiest place on the rugby field to defend from, so we were hoping that maybe we could put him under some pressure in that regard.

James O'Connor was selected at fly-half, for only the second time in his Test career, but that other occasion had been against Wales at the Millennium Stadium in 2011 when Australia had beaten us 24-18, so I knew how well he could do there.

I had been thinking about this Test match since I was 14 years old. Back then, I would be with my twin brother Ben running around the streets of Rhiwbina in Cardiff or pushing weights in the multigym in the garage of our family home. I obviously wanted to play for my school team first, then the district sides up to Wales, but always at the back of mind it was the thought of playing for the Lions in a Test match that inspired me. Now in Brisbane I was about to realise that dream, and be captain as well. It made me feel very humble.

'Since the first team announcement, I have been thinking about it and getting the chance to do it already has been awesome,' I said. 'But I know Saturday will be another level again. I've led Wales out in some pretty big games, but I guess this will blow those out of the water because the Lions is always the pinnacle. It's what you dream about as a young boy, but I'm pretty relaxed at this stage. Any game I play, I don't feel the nerves until match day. This is where we all want to be and the boys not involved have all been very supportive. There's every chance they could get back into the Test team. This is only the first of three Tests. I haven't looked at any press since I've been here; I only worry about what I am in control of.'

And, to make me realise how long my journey had been and how far I had come, in the week of the match I began listening to the same music – for instance the Metallica *Black* album and especially the song 'Sad But True' – as I had done all those years ago. I knew that this was going to be the biggest moment of my career. I thought leading Wales out against France in both the World Cup semi-final in 2011 and in the Grand Slam match of 2012 had been special, but this was going to top them all.

My parents and fiancée Rachel arrived in Brisbane on the

Friday morning before the match and, as I've said, they stayed at my godmother Jane's house along with Dan Lydiate's fiancée, Nia. It is almost difficult to explain how special a weekend this was going to be. It was the stuff of dreams. I was just so proud that I was going to be a Test Lion.

So that's why I had found myself kissing my Lions jersey as I was packing it up for another flight during the week. It was the one I had worn for the first half of my Lions debut against Queensland Reds (we get jerseys for each half and I swapped my second-half ones against Queensland and New South Wales Waratahs with my opposite numbers). And, yes, I had got it washed, but I just couldn't wait to take it home and get it framed for my family.

If I felt like that about those games, imagine how I felt about being presented with my Lions jersey for the first Test – it was mind-boggling. I was hoping that someone special would be brought in to present them to us before the game, just as had happened on previous tours when, say, Willie John McBride did that in Australia in 2001. But I hadn't heard that anything like that was happening, which I think was good because it made the message even more powerful when Sir Ian McGeechan arrived at our team hotel on the Thursday evening to do just that.

For me he was the perfect man to do this emotional job. He is what the Lions are about. His autobiography is called *Lion Man* after all. That sums him up nicely – he is simply a Lions legend. He played for the Lions, appearing in every Test of the 1974 and 1977 tours to South Africa and New Zealand, and he coached the Lions on four tours, to Australia in 1989, to New Zealand in 1993, and to South Africa in both 1997 and 2009. He won two of those Test series, in 1989 and 1997, and he was also an assistant coach to New Zealand in 2005.

We had been told that there was a team meeting at 6pm, and when we went into the team room there he was talking to Gats, and there were the 23 jerseys laid out. I started getting really nervous, and I don't think I was the only one. I was looking around and I could see other players working out how many more people it would be before they got their jersey, and there was some real nervous anticipation. They left me until last. It seemed such a long wait: it was Tom Croft, Jamie Heaslip, then finally me.

I had never met him before, but to look Sir Ian McGeechan in the eye and be presented with my first Lions Test jersey was a truly special moment. He said: 'Good luck. You'll be a great leader.' It was such a simple message, but he really meant it and it made me feel ten feet tall. He had spoken to us all as a group before handing out the jerseys and it was an emotional speech. Leigh Halfpenny was sitting at the front and he was clearly struggling to hold back the tears.

The gist of the speech was that we had been wearing the Lions jersey over the previous few weeks, but now it was going to be different. 'The jersey will come alive,' he said. 'It will demand more from you, as it has demanded more from all the others who have ever worn it.' And that's exactly what I found. You just look at the crest on your chest and it seems to give you an extra 20 per cent. You put your body through things you would not normally do. The stats showed that to be the case. When Ian finished speaking, all the players just burst out into spontaneous applause. He had certainly hit the nail on the head. It was one of the moments of the tour.

Afterwards we were all asked whether we wanted to keep our jerseys or whether we would prefer them to be taken and put out ready in the changing room on Saturday. Some kept them, some gave them back. Me? I was keeping mine! It was my Test jersey and I was taking it back to my room. I went straight there and, before Dan Lydiate came back to the room, I laid it flat out on the bed with the number seven showing. I was so proud.

I thought back to that 2005 replica jersey I'd been given by my parents, also with a number seven on it, and ever since I'd put it away, I'd been dreaming of getting this Test jersey. I stood there staring at it. It was the real thing. I'd done it. I was glad for once that Dan wasn't in the room. It was brilliant to have that nice little moment to myself. I kept turning it over to see which way I preferred looking at it. Then I put it with the number showing again and folded over the part at the bottom on the front that says 'Sam Warburton 1st Test Australia v Lions 22nd June 2013 800'.

As I was about to leave the room, I just had to go back and have another look. There it was, I was going to play in a Test for the Lions, wearing the number seven jersey. I couldn't stop looking at it. That night and the next day I laid it neatly on top of my kit bag with the number seven still showing.

Dan was wearing the number 20 jersey, and he didn't bring

his back to the room. I'm not sure he could trust himself to remember to take it to the ground for a Test! But that's not to say he wasn't immensely proud. Once the match was over, we were both delighted that we were Test Lions. When we got back to the room we kept making T signals to each other. Usually that means a time out, but not here it didn't. It meant that we were Test Lions. We'd been talking about that since 2010, and because Dan had got on, replacing Tom Croft after 72 minutes, we could now both say we had achieved our ultimate ambition. We'd do a double-tap T sign and give each other a wink.

Now we had the shirt, it was time to focus on the game and what we needed to do. As a team and a squad we were so determined to win this first Test, and so take the first step to a series victory.

'Everybody is desperate to achieve this, it is something none of us has achieved and we all desperately want to have it on our rugby CVs,' I said. 'You can see that in the body language. We have Heineken Cup winners, Grand Slam winners, English Premiership winners but nobody has ticked this box. One certainty in all three matches is going to be our determination.'

Another certainty was that I was going to be asked a lot of questions about my captaincy and the way I would go about doing it: 'I try to simplify everything,' I said. 'The occasion is bigger this Saturday, but mentally I will approach it the same. I think changing anything in that way would be the wrong thing to do. I will approach it as any other game, and guys like

Paul O'Connell and Brian O'Driscoll have been making themselves heard this week. They are playing their part as they have done all tour.'

There were loads of good luck messages for the team before the Test, and I was pleased when I bumped into Sir Clive Woodward and met him for the first time as he wished me luck for the Test. I was also touched when I went into the changing room before the match. There were my two jerseys hanging up, and on the bench were my socks and shorts. When I picked up my socks to put them on, there was a little piece of paper underneath them. On it was a lovely message from Will Greenwood, the former England and Lions centre who was out in Australia working for Sky Sports, and who had obviously had access to the changing rooms because of that. I thought that was very nice of him and I've kept that note.

I did not know what I was going to say to the team before we went out. As I've said, one thing I have learnt as captain is not to worry about that sort of stuff. When I started as Wales captain, I sometimes used to plan what I was going to say, but too often when the time came it did not feel natural. So now I just wait until the moment and gauge what I feel needs to be said. For the two games I had been captain on this tour before this, I probably hadn't spoken for more than 20 seconds before the game. This was no different.

I usually sit down on the bench and listen to my music (and I believe there was a camera shot of me doing just that before this match), and I let the louder members of the squad be more vocal in gearing up the boys. I knew that guys like Paul

O'Connell, Brian O'Driscoll and Alun-Wyn Jones would be doing this. Ben Youngs is very good before a game, too. Often I let others have their input and then I will finish things off just before we go out, probably just making three bullet points that will be important for the game. It's no different at half time when most of the chat is tactical, because you are assessing the opposition and what you want to do to combat them. There have to be a lot of leaders on a rugby field these days, and Paulie and Drico are obvious and natural leaders anyway as former Lions captains.

For instance, early on in the Waratahs match we had a penalty and I was about 70:30 in favour of kicking for goal, but I just turned to Paulie and asked: 'Three?' He agreed immediately. It obviously makes sense to lean on these players; I wouldn't just go on my own and make decisions without liaising quickly with one or two of them.

In fact, there is always communication throughout the team. Another example came in the Waratahs match where the front row of Mako Vunipola, Tom Youngs and Adam Jones were constantly feeding me information about the scrummage so that I could talk to the referee about it. In the backs, Jonathan Sexton is also very good at communicating what is going on, as is Jon Davies. Sexto was sometimes called 'the grumpy one' on tour because he is always shouting like hell at training. Some of the boys reckoned that he is the angriest man they have ever met in rugby. But that is a good trait, I reckon. He was only acting like that because he wanted things to be right, and he wanted to help everyone else get things right. In fact, I thought that both he and Owen Farrell were brilliant at organising and bossing the forwards. If they had called a move and you were running the wrong line, they would be the first to scream at you. And that is fair enough.

I tried to make my preparation for this game as close to any other Test match on a Saturday. So that meant trying to keep Thursday and Friday as free of commitments as I could. On those days all I want to do is train, see Rachel and my parents, and spend the rest of my time in the hotel. I might also catch up with my agent, Derwyn Jones, as well as Andy McCann. Along with Dan Lydiate, I met Derwyn on the Thursday before the first Test for a coffee and a chat, and I met Andy, who was out in Australia, on the Friday. Derwyn commented that he had never seen me looking so relaxed and I told Andy when I visited him on the Friday that I felt as ready as I had done before the World Cup semi-final against France and simply could not wait to play. Rarely do I feel like that, but my preparation, both mentally and physically, had been spot on.

I never really want to see anyone else during that period before a Test. So, say, if mates were over in Australia – which they were – I would try to see them from Monday to Wednesday. I'll admit that there was an instance even with the Queensland Reds match where a friend wanted to meet up to collect tickets on the Friday before that match, and, although it was no problem organising tickets for him (which I did), I did make up a bit of an excuse so that I did not meet him. It was just because I wanted to do the team run on that Friday morning, have lunch and then just laze around the hotel getting my mind and body right for the game the next day.

Rachel always says that one of my character traits is that I can be introverted, rather unsociable and be a bit of a loner, and that is just enhanced in the lead-up to a game. So, for example, before the first Test in Brisbane I told my parents and Rachel to come to the family room in the hotel on the Friday so that I did not have to leave the hotel at all.

Sometimes when I've been captaining Wales I might have to go to meet the referee in the evening before a match, which is something I've just had to get used to as captain. But fortunately this meeting often happened earlier in the week on this trip, which helped. I used to find this distraction difficult initially, but it is not a problem any more.

I also have to eat a lot on the day before the game because I really struggle to eat on match days. I will have a lot of food, such as spaghetti bolognaise, chicken breasts, vegetables and even a low-fat apple crumble, as well as plenty of toast and jam as snacks, to make sure that my glycogen levels are high for the game the next day.

As for the game day itself, the kick-offs out in Australia were all late in the evening, so the approach I adopted – as did most of the Welsh boys under the suggestion of Andy McCann – was to split the day into two. That's because if you get up at 9am and start thinking about the game immediately that is an awful long time to be nervous for. To avoid this, I tried to get up as late as I could, but I also had to try to get in three meals, even if that was very difficult for me.

I would normally get up at 10am and have breakfast straight away. I might have to sit down for about 40 minutes just trying to get the smallest breakfast down. I found that I was chewing my food for ages, but hardly anything would go down. Geoff Parling picked up on this early in the tour, because he is very similar. He also finds it hard to eat and he has to make sure he eats a lot to keep his weight up, but even he said that I was unbelievably slow at eating, and most of the other players noticed this and started taking the mick. I would always be the first on a table at meal times and then the last to leave. Fortunately, Leigh Halfpenny is the same, so, when possible, I tried to have match-day breakfast with him.

I was sharing with Dan Lydiate for this Test, so, after breakfast, we went back to the room and put on the TV, watching *Friends*. We would chat normally at this stage, because we would not consider it game day yet, but we would only have a couple of hours before we had to go back downstairs for lunch. There would then be quite a long break before the pre-match meal at about 4.30pm. Quite a few of the boys might go out for a coffee or a walk during that period, but Dan and I are not like that. We prefer to stay in the hotel.

So for the Brisbane Test we went to the hotel outdoor swimming pool, which was on the top of the hotel. We got some Bluetooth speakers that you link up to your phones and, lying on sun loungers in the shade, we listened to some relaxing acoustic music for about two hours. We would still be trying to think about anything but the game at this stage.

After that, there would be a team walk-through when it

would be time to start switching on for the game. In this hotel there was a tennis court where we did that, just doing some line-outs without jumping and some handling drills. It's an exercise just to iron out the creases before the match, as much for peace of mind as anything to make sure you are ready for the game.

After the pre-match meal, there is then about an hour before the team meeting. That is when I really start to ramp it up in terms of my mental preparation. I will have a shower, make sure all my kit is ready and then start listening to my match-day tunes. I will lie on the bed with the TV on, but I am not really watching the TV. Both Dan and I will be staring at it, but will instead be listening to our headphones. It is getting serious then. It is not time for conversations.

If Andy McCann is around with the Wales team, it is at this time between the pre-match meal and getting on the team bus that I would see him. He does motivational videos for me to watch, and he had done some especially for me for this tour, so I would watch them during this period. Having watched one of them and having listened to some motivational music, by the time I walked into the team meeting I was ready to go.

At these meetings, Warren Gatland would speak along with one of the other coaches, Rob Howley, Andy Farrell or Graham Rowntree. It would be time to get on the bus then and there would be silence, with everyone totally focused.

I knew this was going to be a huge game, but when I made that walk from the hotel to the team bus it really did hit home how huge it was going to be. There was a massive crowd of people, chanting 'Lions! Lions!' and screaming for the boys. It was awesome. I hadn't experienced such a reaction to that level before. Normally I would put my headphones on straight away, but this time I kept them off for a while to soak up the atmosphere. From 3pm, from my hotel room, I had been able to hear the fans chanting even with the windows closed. It had just been building for all that time.

As I was walking through the large crowd of fans at the hotel entrance on my way to the team bus, I got a bit of a surprise. A pleasant surprise. I heard Rachel and my mum among them going mental, screaming my name, and then I saw them waving frantically. I had never expected to see them at the hotel. If I had had my headphones on, I would not have heard them. They don't normally do that sort of thing, but I guess they were pumped up too and that was understandable. I went from being nervous to giggling to myself when I got on the bus.

This was the moment when the magnitude of the Lions really hit me, taking me back to the times when I was watching the DVDs and videos of past tours. I just thought 'This is something you want to be a part of.'

So to the game itself. We won 23-21, but what agony it was. We so nearly lost it with the very last kick of the game. That's how close it was.

It certainly began with a bang. More than a bang for the debutant Lealiifano, who was going to have been their goal kicker and who, after just 54 seconds, knocked himself out in trying to tackle Jon Davies. He was actually the first of three

Australian backs to be carried off. Berrick Barnes also went off just before half time after colliding with Folau and Lealiifano's replacement, Pat McCabe, was the third when he departed later after a tackle by Alex Cuthbert.

It was brutal, and the pace of the match was quite incredible, especially in the opening 20 minutes. Referee Chris Pollock gave us an early indication of how he was going to officiate at the breakdown when he penalised Brian O'Driscoll twice in the opening minutes. Thankfully, O'Connor missed both penalty chances from them, and in all Australia missed 14 points with the boot throughout the match, those six plus two more penalties and a conversion. Those misses were to prove vital.

It was tight and it was tense, as both sides looked at each other for the first time in the series and assessed their weaknesses and strengths. It was a time to get the basics right, and I'm not sure either side would have been happy afterwards that they did that or how their tactics went. For instance, our work at the line-out didn't go perfectly. I think everyone agreed that we had perhaps been a little too conservative, often looking simply to win the ball at the front. I usually set myself a target of winning two or three line-outs at the back per match, but in this Test I didn't win one.

After the match, Graham Rowntree and the rest of the line-out committee comprising the likes of Geoff Parling and Paul O'Connell said that in Melbourne for the second Test we simply had to use the back of the line-out more. We had to back our skills more. So there I won two line-outs, as we brought in a couple of calls that involved me. I found myself jumping at the back all week in training, which is something I enjoy, but here the number in my line-out column was zero. This all might sound very obvious, but going into this first Test we had simply wanted to get the fundamentals right. Because we wanted to win ball, we used the front of the line-out a lot, with Jamie Heaslip often going up there, as this was our safest option.

Fortunately, Mike Phillips has such a long pass that you can get away with it. We are coached that when you when you win the ball at the front, you push the ball back to the middle of the line-out, where the scrum half is standing, so that it reaches him as if it were middle ball. Even so, it still gives the opposition openside flanker an extra second of valuable time to get up on your back line, compared with a ball thrown to the back of the line-out, so it is not always ideal.

Australia scored first through Folau. And in fairness it was a quite brilliant try. It was begun by Will Genia inside his own 22, when he took a quick tapped penalty. In such an instance, it is always the case that the defence will be disorganised, so Genia, with Folau outside, could run and run. He did just that until he got near our 22 where, when he was eventually shut down by our defenders, he kicked to his right, where Folau collected to run away and score. O'Connor converted and we were 7-0 down.

Folau had announced immediately that he is a special player. But we had a special wing of our own, and George North soon showed that.

After Leigh Halfpenny had kicked a penalty to make it 7-3, George caught a clearance from Barnes in our own half. He had space and he was already into his stride. He is always very dangerous in that situation. He is unbelievable, an awesome athlete. And you have to remember that he had passed a fitness test on his hamstring only on the Thursday before this Test. He is so good that whenever he catches the ball, I always adjust my running line just to expect a line break and to be on his shoulder. That is how good he is. The tussle between him and Folau was already hotting up, and it became an intriguing part of the series.

So first George swerved outside McCabe, then he managed to avoid O'Connor's ankle tap, before he accelerated away from Barnes and then beat Genia at the corner. It was a stunning try, and I know there was some criticism because he had pointed a finger at Genia after he had passed him, but I know George very well and I am sure there was no malice involved there. He didn't mean any offence. He was just very emotional in such a special moment. He said afterwards that he felt 'horrendous' about what he had done, and I can imagine he did. He is just not that type of bloke to do that sort of thing.

I said to George after the game: 'You do realise that try will be on the reels now for years and years as one of the great Lions tries?' He just laughed. He was a little bit gutted, though, because his partner Becky James, the Olympic cyclist, was in the air, still flying over to Australia, when the game was on. He really wanted her to be there for that try. He said to me that he was hoping to do something similar again in the second Test, so that she could see it in the flesh, as she wouldn't be there for the third Test since she was going to be racing in Portugal. I was certainly hoping he would!

In fact he very nearly didn't have to wait that long as he almost scored again in Brisbane, just four minutes later, after a driving maul from a line-out taken by Alun-Wyn Jones. Mike Phillips passed left to George who went for the corner but, after consultation with the television match official, it was shown that Folau had got a hand under the ball and that George's elbow had been in touch. We still had a penalty, though, and Leigh duly kicked that so that we were 13-7 up. However, we couldn't keep Folau out of the action for long, as he scored another try before the break. This time Stephen Moore and Kane Douglas combined to put him away. O'Connor missed the conversion, though, and it meant that, with Leigh unusually missing a kick just before the interval, we were still 13-12 ahead as we went into half time.

After the match Leigh was actually fined for missing that kick. Now that was harsh! I told you that the fines committee was savage. And they were. It was only his second missed kick of the tour, as he had kicked 25 from 27 at that stage. His conversion of George's try from the touchline had been quite superb. But this was only a bit of fun. And, before anyone says we should not have been doing that sort of thing – fining players for on-field stuff – it was only in jest, and Leigh took it that way.

Leigh is the absolute golden boy. He is always so diligent and organised, spending hours on the laptops reviewing

Alun-Wyn Jones and I tackle Wallaby wing Digby Ioane during the first Test, which began at a brutal and relentless pace. I made 14 tackles in all during the game, according to the official stats.

Trying to evade Wycliff Palu in the heat of the battle in Brisbane.

Thumbs up after a tense victory in the first Test. But I knew there was more to come from the Lions.

Dan Lydiate and I combine to stop Adam Ashley-Cooper getting away during the second Test in Melbourne.

Having been cautious at the line-out in the first Test, we were more expansive in the second one, and it was great to get more involved in this part of the game.

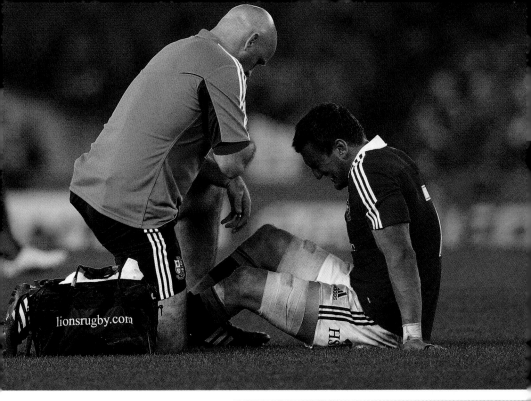

The moment my tour came to an end. I knew immediately there was little chance I would recover in time for the final Test.

I had to be helped off the pitch.

Ben Youngs and I watch on as the Lions lost out by the narrowest of margins to take the series to a decider in Sydney.

One of the most extraordinary moments in the series: George North takes man and ball as he surges forward. Israel Folau can do nothing about it.

Brian O'Driscoll and Warren Gatland work together in training, but it was the coach's decision to leave out the Irish legend from the final Test that caused huge controversy.

While we were at Noosa ahead of the final Test, I could only watch on while the rest of the boys trained.

Mike Phillips, Tommy Bowe, me, Jon Davies, Jonny Sexton, Adam Jones and Ian Evans have some fun at the Steve Irwin zoo, on a day off during the week of the third and final Test.

No stopping the Big Red Machine, as Alun-Wyn Jones calls himself. I thought he was the perfect choice to captain the side in Sydney.

Australia's captain, James Horwill, congratulates me after the Lions had roared to a crushing 41-16 victory at the ANZ Stadium.

The entire squad celebrates a wonderful success – the first Lions series victory since 1997.

Leaving the stadium knowing we had completed what we had set out to do.

There'd been some time to get away from the rugby during the tour, as when we had a barbecue at my godmother's house in Brisbane, but quiet moments were to be few and far between afterwards. Left to right: Dad, Mum, me, Kevin, Jayne, Rachel, Andy McCann, Nia (Dan's fiancée) and Dan Lydiate.

Proudly showing the Tom Richards Cup to the brilliant Lions fans who had given us such support throughout the series, and were rewarded for their efforts with a spellbinding victory.

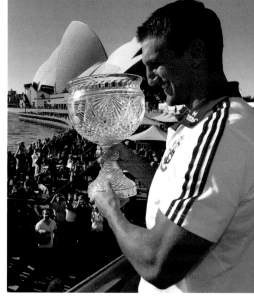

Rachel and I outside 10 Downing Street before meeting David Cameron to celebrate the Lions' victory.

games, and never putting a foot wrong on or off the field. This was about the only thing the fines committee could find to fine him for. His forfeit, like mine for wearing the wrong shoes, was to find his way home from training one day.

Anyway such things were not on our minds as we entered the second half in Brisbane. And Leigh didn't miss another kick, adding a conversion and another penalty in the second half. The conversion came after an excellent and well-worked try from Alex Cuthbert.

It came only eight minutes after the break, and it immediately exposed the cracks in the Australian defence after McCabe had gone off and flanker Michael Hooper had had to play in the centre. Jamie Heaslip won a line-out and from it Cuthie came into midfield off his wing and went around Hooper before going past O'Connor, Genia and Kurtley Beale to score. The television match official confirmed the try, even though some thought Brian O'Driscoll might have blocked O'Connor. He had made some contact but not enough for it to be deemed illegal. He hadn't blocked him. A try it was, and, with Leigh's conversion, it was 20-12.

But soon another O'Connor penalty narrowed the gap to five points, and we were in for a dramatic final half an hour. Nobody was disappointed in that respect. It certainly was dramatic. The replacement Beale kicked two penalties, with one from Leigh for us in between. It was 23-21, with 12 minutes to go.

Five minutes from time replacement Mako Vunipola was penalised at the breakdown for coming in at the side, even though he had been the tackler. We thought that was a harsh decision, but we felt like that a few times that evening, and we lost the penalty count 13-8. Fortunately, Beale missed his shot at goal from 30 metres out.

The two decisions against Brian early on had certainly changed my approach to the breakdown, and I know it did for Brian because he was so scared of receiving a yellow card that he did not commit to rucks after that. Seeing how it was being refereed, I didn't bother competing for the ball on the floor at all. I didn't jackal at all. It was just too risky. You had to be seen very obviously to be supporting your own body weight, or you were in trouble. It was better to try to counter-ruck or get your feet in there.

There was a lot of talk about this afterwards and the way the referee interpreted the rules, but I was fairly philosophical about it. OK, there may have been a couple of decisions that we didn't agree with, but that is the case in any game. We as players make mistakes, so it is only understandable that the referee will make the odd one, too. There are so many things to look out for at the breakdown that it is extremely hard to get the right call every time. I thought Chris Pollock was easy to talk to and I enjoyed working with him.

I thought those early penalties against Brian were harsh, but when he told Chris to look at the replay on the screen, I did think to myself: 'I hope that doesn't get the ref's back up!' I also remember thinking: 'There is no point getting too angry about this. Sometimes there are games when things go against you. There is often nothing you can do. You are not going to change the referee's thought processes. It's a huge game for him, too, and he is not going to change what he is doing halfway through the game.'

It seemed as though we had weathered Australia's final surge, but with just a minute to go we were penalised again, this time at a scrummage. Oh no! It was definitely kickable. It may have been 45 metres out, but it was in front of the posts. This couldn't be happening to me again. In four consecutive matches against Australia in 2012, Wales had lost in the final minutes or so. On the last occasion in Cardiff in December, it had been Beale who had scored the winning try.

He now had the chance to beat the Lions with a penalty. It was some chance for him. He had had his off-field problems and now he was back. He is a top player and I hope he has many highs in his career in the future, but at that moment I'm not sure that was how I was feeling about him, if I'm honest.

What can you do, though? The game was out of our control now. If Beale kicked the penalty, Australia would win. If he missed, we won. That's what it boiled down to. Beale slipped. As he went to take the penalty, his left, non-kicking foot slipped from underneath him and he ended up on his back-side, as the ball went nowhere near going over. It was cruel for him, but it was elation for us. We had won the first Test. It was not time to think about ifs and buts, even if there were plenty. We had won!

It was such a relief. 'That was entertaining, that's for sure,' I said on TV immediately afterwards. 'It was way too close for comfort. That last twenty minutes was so hard. We really had to dig in. Credit to Australia: we can expect a lot more in these next two Test matches.'

The funny thing is, though, I had thought something like this might happen. I'm not trying to say I'm some kind of psychic, but I had thought beforehand about it being a close finish. I'd obviously been involved in all those close finishes for Wales against Australia, and they hadn't gone our way, but before this game I remember thinking that, if it did get close again, then surely it had to go our way sooner or later. And so it did.

Yes, it was close but the good thing was that I thought we had got so much more to give. Physically, I believed we could up the stakes, and there were areas of the game where we knew that we could improve. Our game management may not have been the best, especially in the first half when maybe we tried to play too much rugby. And we had given away too many soft penalties.

Personally, I knew that I could improve too, even if I was reasonably happy with my performance. I had been particularly pleased with how relaxed I had been before the match. I was in an excellent frame of mind going into it. I had made 14 tackles, even if the way the breakdown was interpreted meant that I did not get a turnover.

'It was a heck of a Test match,' I said afterwards. 'And a tiring one, but I felt okay out there. We're battle-hardened because of the warm-up games we've had. We've got some match fitness in our bodies now. It was like last year with Wales all over again. It's out of your control when there's a kick for the opposition in the last minute. It was just a massive delight to win the first game. We've got the momentum and got the ball rolling and now we're just looking forward to next week. They came out well. It's always a quick first twenty minutes and you just have to weather the storm. There are still things to work on, and I think the sides were very evenly matched. It went down to the last ten seconds.'

It was a superb feeling. It was the first time I had beaten Australia and it was unknown territory for me. I was delighted and so happy to have won a Test as captain. It was what I expected to happen, but I still wanted to be ruthless in our preparation for the next Test so we could put the series to bed without the series going to the third Test with all to play for. It is always a great feeling in the post-match press conference when you have won.

It was only the Lions' second win in nine Tests, and the win before that nine began had also been in Brisbane, in 2001. Then, of course, the series was lost after the Lions followed it up with two defeats. We were well aware of what had happened back then. But we had got the win, and I thought, in the end, that we deserved it. We could go to Melbourne with the chance of securing the series.

6

Second Test, Missed Chance

We had won, but victory had come at a cost: Paul O'Connell had broken his arm in Brisbane and was out of the rest of the tour. There was no point dressing it up – it was a massive blow. We would miss him, and I would certainly miss him as a leader. As I've already mentioned, he was such a help to me as captain. And that was why it was important that he stayed on the tour. He could still have a huge input, and I thought that was crucial. That he was so willing to stay and help out said everything about him as a person, and showed that he epitomised everything the Lions is about. But it still did not allow anyone to escape from the reality that we would miss him as a player on the field. His replacement, Geoff Parling, had impressed me a huge amount already on the tour, both as a leader and as an awesome line-out technician, but any side in the world would miss Paul O'Connell.

I never went up to Paulie – or Brian O'Driscoll for that matter – and asked them for help on tour. I hope that doesn't sound bad, but it was rather a case of them coming up to me to offer advice or help. It might even have been just to ask the referee something during a game, but they both helped out, and it was so good to have two great leaders there when I needed them.

For instance, after the first Test I was immediately whisked off to do a live TV interview. While I was doing that, Brian gathered the team around and spoke to them. I thought that was brilliant. I asked some of the players afterwards about what he had said, and they said that it had been a very emotional and passionate speech in which Brian had talked about his experiences in Australia in 2001 as a Lion, when the first Test was won but then the next two Tests were lost and with them the series.

Apparently, he talked about the importance of finishing the job in Melbourne in the second Test and how we would need to improve our performance in order to do that. He said that the players could enjoy the moment of victory, but that we had to back it up and then finish it off. In essence, he was making the point that there had only been one half of rugby played.

Brian was right. But before we could focus on the second Test in Melbourne, there was the last midweek match of the tour to consider – against the Melbourne Rebels, captained by Wales's Gareth Delve. With Paulie out injured, there was a bit of quick reshuffling. Geoff Parling had been due to be captain in that match, but he was now withdrawn from it, leaving Dan Lydiate to be captain and Ian Evans to come in to the second row, and Tom Croft to go on the bench.

In another injury worry from the first Test, Alex Corbisiero had a calf problem, which had forced him off early in the second half. So this meant that the Ulster prop Tom Court, who had been on Ireland's tour of North America but was now in his home city of Brisbane, was called up to the tour party as cover and he went on to the bench straight away for the match against the Rebels, with Mako Vunipola, now likely to start the Test instead of Corbs, withdrawn from the match-day 23.

So, for the first time in Lions history, there were two Welsh captains for a match in Dan and Delve (it was good to see him – he is a top bloke and a fine player), but it was obvious that this was not a run-of-the-mill midweek match with nothing on it. This was a serious chance for players to stake a claim for a Test place. Warren Gatland had emphasised that, had Kurtley Beale kicked one of those two penalties at the end of the first Test, then he might have been considering quite a few changes, so there was no reason why he shouldn't still be thinking about changes.

Usually, you wouldn't even consider playing two matches in such a short space of time, but Lions tours are different, as I've said, and you are always prepared and able to give more of yourself. You will just get yourself through it because you are so desperate for a Test place. I know that for Dan to lead the Lions was probably the greatest moment of his rugby career, but he saw it as an opportunity to use that game as a chance to gain a Test starting spot for the Saturday. I said earlier that he had been delighted with a bench spot for the first Test, but it is the way top sportspeople think that they always want to improve upon things. So Dan wasn't just going to be content with a bench spot now. He wanted to start.

I heard Dan was seriously fired up in the changing rooms before this Rebels game. Adam Beard told me that he almost jumped out of his skin when Dan spoke. He spoke for only about 20 seconds apparently, but he went absolutely mental. It was constructive stuff, of course, but it was said with a real bang. The lads filming the tour DVD would surreptitiously film every captain's speech before the game, so when I heard that from Adam I thought: 'I've got to get hold of this and see it.' I asked Dan about it afterwards and he just laughed it off, as he does.

So eventually Rhodri Bown got it for me and I watched it with him and Rhys Long. It was a bit of a favour for me, because I'm not sure I was supposed to see it. That's why I put the headphones on to listen to it, so nobody else in the team room could hear. I watched it and just said: 'Flippin' heck!' He'd gone nuts, absolutely nuts. It all made sense then, because all those of us not playing were waiting in the tunnel when Dan led the team out that night against Melbourne, and he really did look in a menacing mood. I don't think I've ever seen him looking so fearsome.

Contrast Dan coming out of the tunnel with Simon Zebo. Now he is a joker. He is a seriously talented rugby player, too, but he does like to have a bit of fun. Later in the game that night he produced some magical skill and the crowd were all chanting 'Zebo! Zebo!' and he was cocking his ear to them in recognition. Mind you, there was another moment when they were chanting his name and he was in the defensive line, with the likes of Brad Barritt and Owen Farrell pointing at the players they were marking in the opposition attack, and he was nodding his head and pointing his tongue out at the crowd! What a character! That cracked me up.

There was another story from this game that Conor Murray told, and in fact Zeebs got fined for it. Conor kicked the ball out of play about 30 seconds before the half-time whistle went, thinking that time was up, but that was because Zeebs had been on the floor presenting the ball back, and he had been shouting: 'Kick it out. Time is up!' So Conor did, and then in horror he saw that the touch judge was setting up for a line-out, because there was still time left. He turned around and Zeebs was running off giggling. He had done it on purpose!

Anyway, when the teams were coming out before the start of the match, the boys who were watching from the sidelines said we should keep our hands low. This was the first time I had not been playing when Zeebs was, and when he came out last I realised what they were on about. Apparently, he does it every game: he came out nodding his head and went down low to smack everyone's hands! He just enjoys his rugby so much.

For this game against the Rebels, all those players who had been on the bench for the Test were given a chance, and there was a place for Manu Tuilagi in the centre after injury. Warren explained when the team was announced: 'We've picked a really strong side, with guys who were on the bench last night getting a chance to start. We thought it was important to pick a team that can do a job for us, following on last night's result.

There's still a chance for performances to really catch the eye. We won't think about Test selection until after the match.

'The Brumbies loss was a wake-up call and it will be nice to take more momentum into the second Test. We know the performance in the first Test wasn't brilliant, but it's all about the result. For both sides it was about sparring, finding out information about each other. I'm not sure how much we found out. There were some positive things and some things for us to work on.'

Rob Kearney started at full-back, with Sean Maitland and Zebo on the wings. Brad Barritt partnered Manu in the centre, and Owen Farrell was at fly-half alongside Conor. The front row consisted of Ryan Grant, Richard Hibbard and Cole, and Richie Gray was with Ian Evans in the second row. The back row was Dan, Toby Faletau and Sean O'Brien. It was a seriously strong side, and it gave a seriously strong performance, winning 35-0, with five tries from Maitland, O'Brien, replacement Ben Youngs and Murray, as well as a penalty try when a driving maul was pulled down. Owen kicked three conversions – meaning he had missed just one kick from 17 on the tour – and replacement Stuart Hogg also kicked two conversions.

There were so many good individual efforts that they really did give Warren some selection dilemmas for the second Test. All the back row were excellent, and Richie Gray and Ian Evans had their best games on the tour in the second row. The scrummage went really well and Richard Hibbard carried superbly. Both scrum-halves were really sharp, as was Sean Maitland.

However, for all the success on the pitch that night, there was an incident from the first Test that was attracting a lot of attention. Early in the game, James Horwill's boot had connected with Alun-Wyn Jones's face, for which Alun-Wyn had received a couple of stitches. Warren wasn't happy about that and Horwill was subsequently cited.

'We had a look at it and felt it needed to be referred on,' said Warren. 'I played in the days when rucking was allowed, and I have still got some of the scars that bear witness to the ruckings I had. But the head for me was sacrosanct. You stayed away from that. But it is up to the citing commissioner to make any further decision. Alun-Wyn is fine. The medical team had a look at him at half time, and at full time they put a couple of stitches in his eye.'

At the disciplinary hearing on the Sunday after the Test, Horwill was cleared, but then the International Rugby Board took the unprecedented step to appeal against that verdict. They had never before tried to change a 'not guilty' verdict, although they had acted in 2012 when the New Zealand flanker Adam Thomson had been given a one-week ban for stamping against Scotland, meaning that his ban was increased to two weeks. A new hearing was set for after the second Test, but the verdict was the same, so Horwill did not miss any of the Tests.

I know a lot of people were getting very uptight about this whole saga, which became a big media story, but as players we just couldn't do that. And if the truth be told, we didn't really know much about it at the time. Personally, I hadn't realised that anything might have happened until the day after the game when at breakfast our lawyer, Max Duthie, came up to me to speak about it: 'About the Horwill incident,' he began.

'What Horwill incident?' I asked.

And to be fair, Alun-Wyn Jones didn't make a fuss about it either. Yes, he had some stitches, but that is a fairly common occurrence after games, whether it is from a collision of heads or whatever, but he wanted to play it down. I asked him about it and he just said that he had been on the floor and he had felt something hit his face. He had no idea where it had come from. When you are in a ruck you are thinking of so many things – being aware of opposition bodies coming over, as well as presenting the ball for the scrum-half who is usually shouting at you – that a clip on the head is not something you necessarily notice straightaway. You just get on with it.

I asked Max if I could see the incident, and he showed me there and then on his laptop. It didn't look great, I will admit, and I did think that he would be lucky if he didn't get banned, because the ball was so far away when the incident occurred. But like everyone else among the players I wasn't going to make a fuss.

I certainly didn't have any personal grudge against Horwill. I think he is a really nice guy. He came into our dressing room at the end of the series and we had a good chat about the rest of his season and what we might get up to that night. We talked again later that night when we were both waiting to speak at the official post-series function at the Sydney Opera

House. He was very easy-going and relaxed. Whenever we met for the coin toss before a match, he was always polite and called me by my first name. That's not always the case. Some captains barely look you in the eye when you meet for that, but that is fine by me. Each to their own.

We knew this incident would be taken care of by the disciplinary process, and we had to abide by that and just get on with preparing for the Test. There was nothing we could do to change what happened there, so there was no point in worrying about it. The key for me was trying to stay as relaxed as possible. The tour seemed to be reaching fever pitch, with more and more Lions fans arriving all the time, so it was important not to let all that excitement and anticipation affect us as players.

I'd spent the Sunday after the Brisbane Test at my godmother's house with her partner Kevin and my parents and Rachel. Afterwards, my parents had stayed in Brisbane a bit longer while Rachel came to Melbourne. I was able to have a nice day with her on our day off on the Wednesday before the Test. We had a lovely walk along St Kilda beach and a seafront lunch. It was great just to chill for a while.

It was always easy to do that on this tour. In that respect, it was very different from being at the Rugby World Cup in New Zealand in 2011. There you were based in a hotel for a week, with Wednesday usually being a midweek day off training, where you could sightsee or whatever. Here our days off were mostly travel days, so it made the tour very tough to find down time.

The players take their recovery very seriously in order to give them the best chance of playing well at the weekend. So that often resulted in us just having nights in, relaxing in the hotel. Back home in Cardiff during international campaigns, George North and I will often go to Nando's restaurant to treat ourselves, but in Australia we went to Wagamama's restaurant. One evening off in Sydney, I went to the top of our hotel and sat by the indoor pool looking at the superb views of the city. I lay on a sun bed and listened to a relaxation tape Andy McCann had given me some time before. That is the type of thing I like to do to chill out and rest for the next training day and feel mentally refreshed. It might seem odd not to want to do much when visiting a great country such as Australia, but the focus really does have to be on relaxing rather than all the things one might do if visiting on holiday. After all, this wasn't a holiday.

Happily, on this occasion Rachel and I were able to walk without too much attention. I know there had been stories of some players going out in disguise – and I did once go out in Brisbane with a cap on and my hood up – but it was not too bad. We really did appreciate all the support we received from the Lions fans. George North and I had taken the ten-minute walk to the Adidas store in Brisbane the previous week and we were stopped only a couple of times (they were Welsh fans). It was no problem at all to pose for photos once inside the store, even though it was not a planned visit.

When the side was announced for the second Test, it contained five changes from the first Test. Three of those were

172

because of injury: Paul O'Connell and Alex Corbisiero were out, as I've already said, but so was Mike Phillips, whose knee had been troubling him since the first match of the tour against the Barbarians. 'Mike has been struggling in training and he is such an important player that we want to make sure he is right for next week,' said Warren. 'He could have played, but we have quality in the position.'

Ben Youngs was picked, with Conor Murray on the bench. The other two changes saw Tommy Bowe, whose hand had made a remarkable recovery, come in on the right wing for Alex Cuthbert, and my mate Dan Lydiate come in at blind-side for Tom Croft. The bench was also very different, with only three remaining from the Brisbane Test – Owen Farrell, Richard Hibbard and Dan Cole. In the backs, Cuthie took a place, while Ryan Grant was the loose-head prop replacement and both Sean O'Brien and Crofty provided cover for the back row.

As for Australia they made two changes to their side, both of them because of injury. Kurtley Beale replaced Berrick Barnes at full-back and Joe Tomane, a former rugby league player who had won only one union cap then, came in instead of Digby Ioane on the wing. Christian Lealiifano, who had been carried off in the first minute of his debut in Brisbane, was passed fit to play after the necessary tests for concussion.

'We know Australia will bounce back,' I said. 'They were only a kick away from winning last week, so they know they have got every chance of getting the series back. If it were us who were one-nil down, we would believe we could pull it back. As a nation, they are competitive and optimistic: they will in no way feel down and out. I imagine they will come out firing. It is all or nothing for them. We expect a huge performance from them.'

Brian O'Driscoll had spoken to the team on the pitch in Brisbane, but during the week he also spoke to me and said: 'I think it's worth having a meeting once the team is announced to tell them how we have got to put the series to bed this week and not let it go to the last Test. If Australia win, the momentum will completely swing.' It was good advice, as ever, but I said to him that I thought the message should come from him, because he had been there before in 2001, and that would make it even more powerful. However, he was worried that he had already said this to the players in Brisbane. So I agreed that I would make that speech. Then, when it came to the time of the team meeting, Warren had his say first, and spoke really well, as he always does. And then Brian just took over.

I have to say that it was one of the most unbelievable speeches I've heard. It was done with so much passion that he almost broke down at one stage. It probably lasted only about three minutes, but his words were full of emotion and common sense about the challenge ahead. At the end of it, Warren looked to me to ask if I wanted to add anything. It was just like after Andy Farrell's speech before the Barbarians match in Hong Kong. There was simply no point in trying to follow it. I just tapped Brian on the leg to tell him what a great job he had just done.

The game couldn't come quickly enough after that. I had been counting it down all week. It had been rather strange actually, whereby you would wake each morning and think: 'In five days' time, I could be a Lions series winner.' Then four, then three and so on. There was such a determined mood to wrap things up there and then. It was undoubtedly going to be the biggest game of my life (I know I'd said that about the first Test, too!), the opportunity to win the series and go down in history.

My state was one of nervous excitement. I was nervous because of the massive game ahead, and that is only normal, but I was also excited because of what we were on the cusp of achieving. It was quite difficult to explain exactly how I felt – maybe a bit like a kid at Christmas, who knows Santa is coming but does not know what he is going to get as a present – because this was so different from anything I'd ever experienced before. There was the potential to achieve something that no team had done for the previous four tours, but the challenge of doing that was something we were really looking forward to, and I loved that.

The players were in the squad because they perform well in the biggest games. Normally, you are pretty nervous in the week going into a big game for your club or country, but the feeling ahead of this one was completely different. This really was something special. I felt confident we could do it.

I'd watched the whole of the Brisbane Test back in great detail, and the most obvious thing to me was how much more we could give in terms of our physicality. That had been reflected in Warren's team selection. He wanted more physicality up front. In that first Test, Australia's support players were very quick to get to the rucks to help the ball carrier. It made it very difficult for us then to compete and slow the ball down. The breakdown in Melbourne was going to be key, especially as Craig Joubert was refereeing. He would allow more of a contest there. He likes speed of ball and is always clear in his instructions. If we could get that part of our game, and the scrummage, right, then there was a good chance we could win the game.

Unfortunately, Warren, Graham Rowntree and I nearly blew our chances of building a good relationship with the referee when we turned up late for our meeting with him. We had a nightmare going across Melbourne to meet him on the Wednesday before the Test. We were supposed to meet him at 5.45pm, but at that time we were still in our Land Rover with our driver, one of our security guys, Ray Clark, struggling with the Satnav system on the vehicle. And we were there for a lot longer after that, as we had to text Craig quite a few times to apologise, and we also had to rearrange our squad meeting back at our hotel, where the team for the Test was to be announced.

We ended up being in the car for an hour and ten minutes, which meant that we were an hour late for our meeting with Craig. It was unusual that Graham was with us – the first time I could remember another coach other than the head coach being there – but he wanted to go through a few scrum engagement calls with Craig.

Second Test, Missed Chance

At least it gave Graham time to talk to me about the selection that was to be announced when we got back. He said that we were going to try to physically dominate Australia. 'Your mate Lyds is playing,' he said. I remember thinking how awesome that was. I was actually a bit like a dad or brother at that moment. I was so proud for Dan. I knew how much it would mean to him, and I couldn't wait to see his face when he was told when we got back. This is no disrespect to Tom Croft, who, of course, was gutted to be left out of the starting team and alongside whom I'd really enjoyed playing in the first Test, but I was so pleased for Dan.

It's no surprise that I like playing alongside him. He can do his famous chop tackles and then I can jackal. It is not always that I make jackals immediately from Dan's tackles, but I definitely find I make fewer tackles when Dan is playing, so that does free me up to try to win turnover ball at the tackle areas. If I had to pick a six to play alongside it would be Dan, simply because we have an understanding and relationship that has been forged over quite a long period on and off the field.

In the Land Rover, Gats also told me that Tommy Bowe was going to be starting. That was another big call, because Alex Cuthbert had scored in the first Test after all, but it was felt that Tommy's defensive qualities and his experience of the big occasions gave him the nod, and he was in.

The call with Mike Phillips was less of a surprise, even if it came as such to those outside of the camp. He simply had not trained all week because of his knee, but had been in the pool instead. He had been struggling since injuring it in the match against the Barbarians in Hong Kong and had been icing it after every match and every session. To be fair to Mike, I have never seen him work as hard as he did during this period. He has had some unfair press over the years, but up until the third Test he was as professional as any player I have ever seen. He desperately wanted to make sure that he was fit for that last Test, because he was probably thinking that he might never have another chance in a Lions shirt. It was mentioned by quite a few of the boys how hard he was working, and was, I suppose, testament to what the Lions means to any player. As someone said: 'If Phillsy is doing all these extra sessions, then it really is time to get our heads on!'

Graham took his laptop with him and showed Craig some calls and some contact-area clips. He would ask questions such as: 'If you see that, Craig, what are you going to do?' It was just a case of us wanting to know where we stood, because different referees can see the same action in different ways, so it is vital to understand what to expect of the man in charge. We cleared up about the release of the tackled player and if the arriving player was part of the tackle. We had obviously had problems at the contact area in the first Test, and we wanted to be able to go back and tell the players exactly what Craig wanted. As it was, we won two turnovers in the opening stages of the Test, so that definitely worked.

We also wanted to talk to Craig about blocking. The Australians – and that is all their teams and not just the national team – are quite cute in how they help their back three counter-attack after a long kick. The players retreating will cleverly run lines that the counter-attacker can run into. He will run straight at one of his own players so that a hole is created. It is difficult for the referee to pick this up, so we were asking that the touch judges watch out for this a bit more.

In fairness, I thought all the officials ended up having really good games here in Melbourne. I've always got on well with Craig, as has Gats, and I enjoy having a chat with him after games. In fact, if I had to pick one referee whom I find it easiest to deal with, I would say Craig Joubert.

When we had finished talking to Craig, we were inevitably still running late for our meeting back at our hotel, and I was to pay for that because it had been decided to conduct a fines meeting while the players were waiting. I walked in late and all the boys said: 'You've got to do your fine, Warby. You've got to roll the dice.' I had been fined because it had been thought that I got Christian Wade's name wrong. I hadn't, but when somebody said during training before the Test: 'Christian is over there,' I had replied: 'Who's Christian?' because I was looking at the Test squad and there was no one called Christian in that.

'That's shocking that the tour captain doesn't even know one of the players' names,' they said. 'Christian Wade!'

'Ah Wadey,' I replied. 'He's over there behind the posts, not with the Test squad.' But it had no effect. I was fined, and there's no arguing with the fines system. Because I had come in late, I did not know what any of the forfeits were. So I rolled the dice and it landed on a four: the room went berserk. With all the management in there too, there were about 80 people present, and there were people standing on chairs screaming and others throwing things. Whatever it was that I had to do, everyone was clearly very happy with it. I looked up on the board next to number four and it said: 'Ring up your club coach and ask him to be captain next season.'

Nightmare. My heart sank. This was probably worse for me than anyone else. Simon Zebo had had to do it earlier, but, with all due respect, and with the leaders Munster have, the coach would have cottoned on to that one fairly swiftly! This was a conversation our director of rugby at Cardiff Blues, Phil Davies, was expecting to have with me in the very near future. I had spoken to Phil before the start of the 2012-13 season and said that I did not really want to be captain for region and country.

So now I had to phone up Phil in front of the whole squad. I had to plug my phone into an iPod docking station and talk on the speakerphone so that everyone in the room could hear. It was so awkward. He answered and I asked him how he was and how his family was. Then I said: 'Look, I think I've moved on from last season and I'd like to be captain this season for the Blues. I'd like to stick my hand up for it.'

There was then a silence during which everyone in the room was trying so hard not to laugh. Phil then rather hesitantly said: 'Ah, OK.'

I then replied: 'I've got to go, I'll text you later.' It was the most horrendous conversation I've ever had to have. Everybody in the room was going mad again now. But then suddenly the room fell silent because Gats said that the fines meeting was over and it was time to announce the Test team. I have never seen the mood change so dramatically in any room.

Anyway as soon as the meeting had finished, I ran back to my room to phone Phil. He'd already sent a text saying: 'Was that you who phoned me?' So I think he knew that it was not a normal conversation. He was fine about it, and I did say to him that it was one of the funniest things that had happened on tour and it was bound to be on the tour DVD, so at least he would be on that.

With all that preparation behind us, and everyone focused on the task in hand, it was time for the second Test to begin. To sum it up in a few words: we did pretty well at the breakdown, the scrummage did not go that well, especially in the first half, we lost the game 16-15 and I pulled my hamstring with 14 minutes to go. That in a nutshell is how the second Test went. It was agony for me in so many ways.

Let's deal with the injury first. I was jackaling on Australia's replacement flanker, Liam Gill. Something similar had happened once or twice in the last couple of seasons where my legs had gone straight and I had been hit, and I'd recognised at the time how lucky I was to have escaped without any serious damage being done. But this time I had no such luck. I fell backwards and, as I did so, I realised I was in trouble, and then the last and third of the Australians to the breakdown, replacement prop James Slipper, came in and finished me off. I could feel it coming, but I just couldn't do anything about it. He hit me and that was that. My left hamstring had gone. He'd not done anything wrong; it was just the position I was in when he caught me that did the damage.

I managed to get up, but I was in serious pain and I could only hobble. I raised my arm to the bench to signify that I was injured. The problem was that the ball was still in play. I had to try to stay in the defensive line until it went out. Dan Lydiate was screaming for me to do just that, as was Alun-Wyn Jones. In fairness Alun-Wyn had walked the walk in that respect a couple of years before, when he had dislocated his shoulder against England. He'd done the damage to his right shoulder and he got back in the line and made a huge hit with his left shoulder! With Wales, our defensive coach Shaun Edwards is always insisting: 'You've got to get back in the defensive line unless you've got a broken leg.' And Andy Farrell is of the same mind-set. Perhaps the fact that they both learned their rugby at Wigan is something to do with it!

My leg wasn't broken, so I had to try. Three times I went down to the ground in pain, but then I just about managed to get myself back up to try to make a tackle. I could do little as Michael Hooper went through. In the end, it was a relief when Kurtley Beale knocked on and I could receive attention. There was simply no way I could carry on. I remember my mum once saying that if I go off the field, I'm always out for a while, as I never go off unless I have to. I remember the physio and doctor asking me if I wanted a stretcher, to which I replied: 'No chance! I'll walk off!' I don't want to look like some football players do who get stretchered off for a slight injury!

Second Test, Missed Chance

All I could do was hope that we could hold on. We were 15-9 up at the time. Up to that point, it had been a topsy-turvy game. We had begun really well, and I opted to kick a penalty to the corner so that we could use the 13-man line-out tactic that Wales had used so effectively against New Zealand in the previous autumn. We surged towards the line, but the Australians defended it really well.

Little did I know it at the time, but I think that was the crucial moment of the match. It's hard to say, but I believe that, had we scored then, the result might have been very different. We did eventually get a penalty from that pressure, which Leigh Halfpenny kicked after unluckily hitting the crossbar earlier, after I'd had a good start to my game by winning a penalty at the breakdown from James Horwill.

We did a lot of good stuff in the opening 20 minutes, but it was not rewarded on the scoreboard. So Australia led 6-3 after 23 minutes through two Christian Lealiifano penalties, both of which were given against Mako Vunipola for collapsing at the scrummage. It was not all one-way traffic in there, as Mako soon sorted out any issues there were, and he, Tom Youngs and Adam Jones made sure that we then won two penalties, which Leigh kicked, to put us 9-6 ahead. Mako got some stick after this game apparently, but after some initial troubles, I thought he had a really good game, making 15 tackles and also gaining a turnover.

It was 9-9 four minutes before half time when Dan Lydiate was penalised for offside, and Lealiifano kicked the penalty. It looked like Dan was a little over-eager in defence, but, after reviewing the video analysis, he had actually showed great line speed and was onside. It is a huge strength of his, but he can often spook referees, hence the penalty decision here. We regained the lead just before the break. Leigh's high kick was chased and collected by George North. From there, the ball was spread wide and Jamie Heaslip carried really well before Ben Mowen was penalised for holding on at the tackle. Leigh made no mistake and we were 12-9 ahead at the interval.

The period after half time was hugely intense. It was also a period in which I thought I found my best form of the tour, which made my injury even more disappointing. I felt that I had a good game and was really happy with my overall performance. Throughout my tour, I believed my game was improving with every match I played. And here I felt I was back to where I should be, especially in that early part of the second half.

I said to myself before the tour that I wouldn't read any press and I hadn't really done until after this Test, when my dad sent me some comments that Sir Clive Woodward had made about my performance. He said it was 'the most outstanding performance I have ever seen from a Lion'. Wow! I couldn't believe that. That is one of the biggest compliments I've ever been paid.

But it would have felt even better had we won the Test. Just before I went off, Leigh had kicked another penalty after we had caused Australia all sorts of problems at a scrummage. The passage of play leading to that scrummage will be remembered for a long time. It was the moment when George North performed a fireman's lift on Israel Folau. What made it so remarkable was that George had the ball, not Folau. Brian O'Driscoll had passed the ball through his legs to George and when Folau had tried to tackle George, he had just picked him up on his shoulder and ran with him. It was a stunning piece of physical strength.

So, with 17 minutes to go, we led 15-9. I think when I went off, Warren Gatland had been just about to bring Dan Lydiate off. Dan had had a magnificent game, making tackle after tackle, but his legs had gone a little by then, which was not surprising given that he had played against the Melbourne Rebels in the week. He had to stay on, though, and, with Sean O'Brien already having replaced Jamie Heaslip, Tom Croft replaced me.

Australia now threw everything at us. Will Genia started running the show and his work took his side close to our line. There they took a scrummage instead of a penalty and then pounded away at our line. They went through 14 phases, and even though it seemed that Mako's tackle had stopped Genia, the ball was put left and Adam Ashley-Cooper scored. The conversion for Lealiifano was not simple, just about seven metres in from the touchline, and he duly nailed it to put Australia 16-15 ahead.

But the game was not over. Far from it.

There were nerves and errors galore. Australia kicked the ball out after taking it into their 22, but we then lost the line-out. And then there were only seconds left when Australia were penalised for holding on in our half. We tapped and drove on a couple of times, and then Australia were pinged again, just around the halfway line, still just inside our half. Leigh had a chance at glory, but the truth was that it was an almost impossible kick.

We were all praying that he might manage it. Quite literally. As Geoff Parling said afterwards: 'Look, I'm not a religious man, but I was almost praying for him [Christian Lealiifano] to miss [the conversion of Adam Ashley-Cooper's try] and then sending a little prayer for Pence to knock that last one over. Leigh was like everyone else, absolutely devastated.'

Indeed he was, but he had no reason to be. He had still kicked 32 out of 36 kicks on tour up to that point, but this was one that he would not normally have tried to take on had it not been for the situation we were in, with time up. When Leigh stepped up for the kick, it's very hard to explain how I felt. I didn't know whether I would be celebrating a series win or picking the lads up for next week, but I knew I would find out within the next 20 seconds. It was incredible excitement. When we lost the game, I realised I had to be brave and positive to help guys prepare for the third Test, whatever my own injury situation.

I've seen him kick them, of course, especially in training, but on this occasion he didn't quite connect with it. It was, though, a realistic chance of winning the Test series. We had to go for it. Had I been the captain on the field at the time, I too would have looked at Leigh and asked him to go for it, as Brian O'Driscoll, who had taken over as captain, did.

I know Leigh so well and I knew he would be blaming

himself. He is so professional and so selfless that that is just the way he always thinks. I also realised that he would recover from it. He had been like this after he had missed another long-range kick from near halfway in the World Cup semi-final in 2011 against France, but he had come back. In fact he had won the first match of the 2012 Six Nations out in Ireland with a pressure kick. Mentally he is so strong.

We hadn't lost here because of that miss. We hadn't been good enough on the night in many other areas. I mentioned that I thought the first 20 minutes had been vital. But there were other factors: we hadn't made one line break throughout the game, having made six in Brisbane. Overall in the match here, the Australians had carried 420 metres with the ball; we had made just 148. In attack we had just not been good enough.

'We're going through what Australia went through last week,' I said immediately after the match on TV. 'The boys will realise we've still got a Test series up for grabs. There's some good stuff in there. We're definitely capable of winning the Test series. It's going to be won by a whisker next week and I hope it's us. Australia got hold of us when they got territory in our twenty-two and we found it difficult to get out. It's much easier said than done. Territory is everything in games like this. Australia came away with points and that's everything.'

I was obviously asked about my injury: 'I felt something in my hammy,' I said. 'I've put some ice on it, and the physios will assess it in twenty-four hours' time. Fingers crossed.'

I knew that it was not good, but publicly I still had to cling on to any last hope at this stage. 'I have a sore hamstring at the moment,' I said at the press conference afterwards, when I was asked about it again. 'The normal protocol is ice every two hours throughout the night. The physios never make a proper assessment until twenty-four to forty-eight hours, so on Monday I should know what's going on. I haven't done this injury before. Normally, if I've tweaked a knee I know what it is, but this is a new injury. Of course I want to lead the team in the third Test and I'll do everything I can to do that.'

Warren obviously wasn't happy with our performance, especially in the last quarter: 'It's just about game management,' he said. 'That's what Test match rugby is about – a couple of crucial line-outs, a couple of crucial turnovers and even when they made mistakes and the ref said "advantage over", we haven't made the most if it. We were pretty comfortable at half time, but they never give up and it went their way. We weren't smart enough and didn't look after the ball well enough.'

I had been utterly convinced that we would win that game. I remember speaking to one of the guys doing the tour DVD that morning. He asked me how I felt and I told him that I wasn't as nervous as I had been before the first Test. 'I can't see us losing,' I said. I genuinely thought we would win that day, and so win the series. And I'm pretty sure that all the other players felt the same way.

That said, though, the series was still drawn at 1-1. It wasn't over. That needed to be said, and it was said in the changing rooms afterwards by both myself and Gats. Our messages

were very similar. We both said that we were in the same situation as we had been that morning. We needed to win one
game to win the series. 'It will just have to be a bit more
dramatic now,' I said. 'It will be a big finale now, and we will
enjoy it even more. In seven days' time, we will be cracking
open the champagne.'

It was quite hard for me to say these things, because I knew
that I wouldn't be involved because of my injury. Somewhat
ironically, I had said to the players before the game that it did
not matter if they put themselves through so much that they
were injured and could not play the following week. It was all
about there and then, I said. 'It's all about sacrificing yourself
now and making sure we win,' I said. Sadly, I had done that,
but we hadn't quite won.

Yes, there was the thought that the momentum could have
swayed Australia's way, but I genuinely did not think that was
the case. In fact, as soon as this Test had finished, I remember
thinking that we would win the last Test. I believed that the
Australians had expended so much emotional energy in
winning that match – captain James Horwill was in tears on
the field at the end – that I was not sure they could reach
those levels again. I know Warren thought the same, and he
said so publicly later in the week. So that was my message
afterwards.

It had not been a good day. Gutted, I went back to the team
hotel where I met my parents and Rachel. We chatted for a
while, but I was not really up for too much talking. Soon I said
to my parents: 'I'm going to go to my room and get some

food.' They understood, but as I was just about to leave, my mum said: 'Come here a second, I've got something to tell you.'

I knew immediately what it was. 'Gus has gone, hasn't he?' I asked.

He had. Gus was my beloved Shetland sheepdog, named after Gus Poyet, the former Spurs footballer (we have another one called Teddy, after Teddy Sheringham). He had died on the Thursday before the match, and my parents hadn't told me until after the game because they hadn't wanted to distract me, as they knew how much he meant to me. He had not been well, and, as I was leaving for the tour, I had been in the car with Rachel when I asked her if we could go via my parents' house. She pulled up outside and I rushed inside.

There was no one there, but Gus and Teddy were. I wanted to say goodbye to Gus, just in case he went downhill while I was away. I had a feeling that it might be the last chance I would have to see him. I got back in the car, and Rachel asked what I had been doing, though I think she knew. 'Saying goodbye to Gus,' I said.

My twin brother, Ben, had been trying to keep him going at home until I got back, but sadly that didn't happen. I'll admit that my emotions got the better of me when my mum told me. I couldn't hold it back. I was not in a good place. We'd lost the Test, my hamstring had gone, and now so too had Gus.

7

Third Test, Lions Glory

Did I know my tour was over the moment I injured my hamstring? In short, yes. Sometimes you never know, because you do these things and they feel more painful than they actually are. And I did think for a second: 'Maybe it is a one- or two-weeker and I can rush back.' But, if I am honest, I always thought deep down that I was struggling. I've seen guys with grade-one tears to their hamstring walking about reasonably comfortably afterwards. I was not like that; I was really struggling to walk.

Hamstring injuries can be complex and they often need more time to recover. I had a scan in Melbourne on the Sunday after the Test and stayed there with Eanna Falvey, one of the team's doctors, while the rest of the squad moved on to Noosa on the Sunshine Coast. As I went for my scan, there were so many press people and cameras in the hotel reception. They must have been there all day, waiting for me to go for that scan. I didn't realise how big a deal it was, and I said this to Eanna, to which he replied: 'You are the Lions captain!' I guess it still hadn't sunk in.

The cameras were still there when we got back, but we drove into the hotel via a private access as I did not want them to see me disappointed, as by then I knew the bad news. And it was conclusive, and sad, news. It was a significant tear, so I was out of the last Test, but by then I had prepared myself for that. The doctors and management asked me when I wanted to release the news, and I said that we might as well do it straight away. It was going to be pretty hard to hide the scale of my injury when I was walking around on crutches!

So on Monday 1 July a press release was sent out. It said: 'The British & Irish Lions confirmed today that captain Sam Warburton would play no further part in the tour after suffering an injury during the second Test. Warburton remained in Melbourne after the match under the supervision of Lions team doctor Eanna Falvey to undergo a full medical assessment and a scan confirmed a significant tear in his left hamstring.

'Warburton, who will remain with the tour party for the third Test in Sydney on Saturday, said: "It is incredibly disappointing to be ruled out of the tour through injury as we head to Sydney for the deciding match. I wish the team all the best and hope I can play some part in the build-up this week. I am confident that the boys can finish the job off and secure the series win."'

Initially, of course, there was much despondency, not helped by the result in Melbourne and Gus dying, too. But I became much more philosophical after lots of reflection over the days that followed. If, at the start of the season, someone had told me I would start two Lions Tests, and as captain too, I would have bitten their arm off.

That Sunday night, as I was the only player left in the team hotel in Melbourne, I had a nice private meal with Rachel and my mum and dad. And they all told me how proud they were of me, which made me feel better. I realised that I was very fortunate. I did not feel as if it was the end of the world then. I was still going to be there for the boys in the last Test, and I was hoping that when we won, I would be there to celebrate with them. It could have been worse. That's how I was thinking.

I was proud of what I'd done, and of how I had played in that second Test. I think I had made an impression. That was why I was pleased to receive a text from Will Genia, the Australian scrum-half. I've always found him a really nice guy, and we have always shaken hands and had a chat after matches. He is managed by the same agency as some of the Lions players, so he had got my mobile number through that, and he sent a message saying: 'Bad luck on your injury. They will miss you.' Just like Chris Robshaw's message to me after the Lions squad announcement, that meant a lot to me.

This was going to be a strange week. It was similar to the 2011 World Cup in many ways, where I couldn't play in the third-place play-off against Australia because I was banned after being sent off for my tackle on Vincent Clerc against France in the semi-final. I was still in the camp then, but couldn't play. Although I have to say this was obviously on a much grander scale. This was like a World Cup final in Sydney now.

Before the final Test, I joined the rest of the squad in Noosa for a few days of rest and recuperation. Warren Gatland had been there the year before to check it out and had decided, with no midweek game, it would be the perfect place to begin the last week of the tour. Had we won in Melbourne, I suppose it would have been where we celebrated. As it was, it was where we chilled. Not that it was a universally popular move. Sir Clive Woodward, for one, considered it a bad idea and said so in his newspaper column, writing: 'It was a big mistake to jump on a two-and-a-half-hour flight to the Sunshine Coast on the morning after a Test match. These guys are battered and bruised, but you do not need to fly to Noosa to get some rest and rehabilitation. It is the last place I would take the team.' I have to say that I disagreed with that and thought it was a really good idea all along.

There was no need to do a great deal of training that week. Players can switch off and back on. If you wanted someone to turn up on a Friday to do a session before a Saturday game, they could do it. You don't necessarily have to do all the work in the week, all the time. By this stage, the boys' bodies were hanging on. This was at the end of a very long season, remember, let alone the bruising impact of the tour itself. By then, everyone knew the calls and their roles. The team run before the second Test had lasted only 12 minutes, and it was the sharpest one we had had all tour.

Noosa was all about freshening the players both physically and mentally. It was good for everyone to get away from the spotlight. It was perfect. The beaches were lovely and there was plenty of surfing and jet skiing. Not that I could do any of that with my injured hamstring. I was sharing a room with Leigh Halfpenny, and he would come back to say, 'Yeah, just been surfing' or 'Just been swimming in the sea'. I saw a story in a local newspaper that a 6ft bull shark had been found washed up on the beach in Noosa and apparently it had been chased in by a bigger shark! This freaked me out, and I swore never to go in the sea there. I showed this story to a few of the boys to try to put them off, but they didn't care!

I couldn't do anything, because I was on crutches for the first two days in Noosa. It was a little bit boring for me, because all I could do was ice my leg. But we were leaving on the Wednesday and, despite the shark story, I eventually thought to myself: 'I've just got to go in the sea'. So I did; I went there with all the other boys after training, and really enjoyed it. I just had to make sure that I kept my injured leg straight and I was OK.

There was also time to go to the cinema during our stay and I went with Leigh, George North, Dan Lydiate, Richie Gray, Ryan Grant and Stuart Hogg to watch the Brad Pitt film *World War Z*. And I even made a trip to the zoo, with Tommy Bowe, Mike Phillips, Ian Evans, Adam Jones, Jon Sexton and Jon Davies. It was my first real trip out on the tour. Despite all that, I think the main attraction was the ice-cream parlour. One day I went there with George North, Richie Gray and the two analysts, Rhys Long and Rhodri Bown.

We thought we were being a little bit sneaky by popping out there, but then we poked our heads through the door and we saw the likes of Owen Farrell and Mako Vunipola in there. There were about ten of the boys in there already! So I thought I'd have a double Knickerbocker Glory with double chocolate, chocolate flake and chocolate sprinkles! I am a bit of a chocoholic after all. That cheered me up. It was off-season for me now, unfortunately. Had I been playing in the third Test, I don't think I would have touched the ice cream, even though I don't put weight on easily. In this instance, I knew I would not be playing for some time, so it was time to ease back a little on the strict diet.

Everyone was relaxed, but it could not last. There was a Test match to be played in Sydney, and there was a team to be picked for it. It was a selection that was to cause rather a fuss – and that's putting it mildly. There were six changes from the side that had started the second Test in Melbourne.

This is the press release that would send reverberations around the British and Irish rugby world: 'Alun-Wyn Jones will lead the British & Irish Lions against the Qantas Wallabies in the 3rd Test at ANZ Stadium in Sydney on Saturday. Ospreys lock Jones replaces the injured Sam Warburton in a team showing six changes to the one that started last Saturday's 2nd Test in Melbourne. Sean O'Brien takes over from Warburton, Jamie Roberts replaces Brian O'Driscoll in the centre and scrum-half Mike Phillips has recovered from a knee injury to start instead of Ben Youngs. Alex Corbisiero returns from injury to replace Mako Vunipola, who moves to the bench, Richard Hibbard makes his first starting appearance at hooker, while Toby Faletau makes his Test debut at No. 8.

Third Test, Lions Glory

'British & Irish Lions Tour Manager Andy Irvine said: "It has been a great tour on and off the field. The hospitality we have received from the Australian people has been outstanding. The banter between the fans has been in great spirit and to date we have had two incredibly exciting Tests. It is amazing that the last three series between the Lions and the Wallabies have gone down to the last Test. In 1989 the Lions triumphed, in 2001 it was the Wallabies who won the series, and now in 2013 we go to ANZ Stadium in Sydney with the series and the Tom Richards Trophy up for grabs. There is nothing between these two teams, with the last two Tests being decided in the dying moments. The Test is a sell-out and the whole rugby world is looking forward to the match with great anticipation."

'Head Coach Warren Gatland said: "It all comes down to Saturday. Winner takes all. We know we can leave nothing in the tank and that only a complete performance will get us across the line. Picking this team was not easy and ultimately with several players available after recovering from injury, the head overruled the heart in many selection decisions. It has been a challenging tour and we have had our fair share of injuries but we always knew that would be the case. Brian O'Driscoll is a great player and has had a wonderful career, but for the final Test in Sydney we just felt Jamie Roberts' presence offered us something more. Mike Phillips and Alex Corbisiero were 1st Test selections and would probably have played in the 2nd Test if not for injury. Richard Hibbard, Toby Faletau and Sean O'Brien have also earned their starting places."'

It is worth reiterating what was happening here: Sean O'Brien was taking my place on the openside flank, Mike Phillips was returning from injury to take over from Ben Youngs at scrum-half, as Alex Corbisiero was instead of Mako Vunipola at loose-head prop. Richard Hibbard was being preferred to Tom Youngs at hooker, and Toby Faletau to Jamie Heaslip at No. 8.

Then there was the call that created the biggest fuss: not that Jamie Roberts was coming into the side after recovering from injury, but the fact that he was replacing Brian O'Driscoll. Brian was many people's choice to replace me as captain, but instead Alun-Wyn Jones was made skipper. On the bench were Tom Youngs, Mako, Dan Cole, Richie Gray, Justin Tipuric, Conor Murray, Owen Farrell and Manu Tuilagi. So there wasn't even any room for Brian O'Driscoll there, either.

As I've said before, I try not to read too much of the press, but in this instance it has been difficult to avoid what was being said and written then. There seemed to be uproar that Brian had been dropped. And I will admit I was surprised, too, that he had been dropped. I thought that his experience would be a big factor and that the selectors would go with that.

But on the flip side, you had to consider how well Jon Davies was playing. He had played inside centre in the first two Tests, with Brian, but that is not Jon's preferred position. Jamie Roberts was coming back into his usual inside-centre berth, so, with Jon moving outside, it was seen as Jon who was the man keeping Brian out. I thought Jon was one of the stand-out players of the whole tour. I actually think that he is still going through a spell that is similar to that once experienced by Dan Lydiate.

In other words, for some reason people are struggling to come to terms with how good Jon really is. Dan had been putting in consistent world-class performances for a long time before people started realising that. And Jon has been doing the same for Wales ever since Tom Shanklin retired in 2011. If you watch the games closely, he is nearly always one of the best players on the field. I'm not sure people realise how big and physical he is. He showed that when he ran into Christian Lealiifano in the first minute of the first Test. He is one of the strongest players in the Wales squad, and he weighs in at a hefty 106kg. I think he is someone who would have surprised the players from the other countries in the Lions squad. Seeing him up close for the first time, they would have suddenly noticed how big, physical, quick and skilful he is. He has got all those attributes, and from now on I suspect a lot more people will realise that.

I had no idea that Brian was going to be dropped, but I do remember being in the team room there in Noosa before the announcement was made. I was talking to Jamie Roberts, who was playing table tennis at the time and was obviously nervous about the announcement. Having missed the first two Tests because of his hamstring injury, he was desperate to play. And I was hoping that was going to be the case for him. He had worked very hard to get back and I knew that he would make a big impression if he was picked. He is such an important and influential player.

Jamie is normally quite loud and confident, but he was rather quiet and reserved at this moment. It was a strange atmosphere in that half an hour before the side was announced. I also saw Brian sitting on his own and he was very quiet. Looking back with the benefit of hindsight, it makes sense now. He had already been told that he was not going to be involved, and it was right that he had been told beforehand, just out of respect. That doesn't usually happen, but in this instance it was right. Brian is a rugby legend.

There seemed to be a lot of other arguments that then seemed to flow from people's anger at Brian's dropping. For instance, the fact that there were now ten Welshmen (Leigh Halfpenny, Jon Davies, George North, Jamie Roberts, Mike Phillips, Richard Hibbard, Adam Jones, Alun-Wyn Jones, Dan Lydiate and Toby Faletau) in the starting line-up worried some. Even though I wasn't playing, I got dragged into it, too, with Willie John McBride, the captain of the 1974 Lions, saying that I shouldn't have been captain in the first place.

I didn't read or listen to much of what was being written and said at the time, but I have since caught up with a lot of that. 'I was absolutely gutted,' said Willie John. 'The first thing that came into my mind was that Robbie Deans, the Australia coach, must be laughing all the way. The Australian media have convinced him [Warren Gatland] to drop O'Driscoll, which I find amazing, I must say. He was the guy I would have picked as captain of the tour. He has been a big influence on the tour, but you live and die by the team you pick, so we will see what Saturday brings.'

Then there was the former Ireland captain Keith Wood: 'Brian O'Driscoll has been quiet in the two Tests,' he said. 'But at every stage, he has been the clarion call once Paul O'Connell got injured. I just think Gatland has made a terrible mistake.'

In response to that, I just go back to what I said at the start of the book. I feel that I was the right man to captain the Lions on this tour. All the people who said that you needed experience of having been on a Lions tour before didn't really know me as a character. I am different from a lot of other players. I am relaxed, and I knew that I could do a good job. I knew that I could treat a Lions Test just as another game of rugby, for that's what it is when you strip it down.

Of course, I was aware of what the Lions means and I hope I have already articulated how much it means to me, but I also knew that once we were actually on the rugby field I could play and make decisions as if it were any other Test match. I think that was why Warren picked me. Looking back now, we won the Test series and I'd like to think that I did a decent job.

Brian, of course, was magnificent about being dropped. As I just mentioned, Warren had made sure that he spoke to him before the team announcement, and I think Brian appreciated that. He congratulated Alun-Wyn immediately and after training that day he asked Jamie Roberts if there was anything extra he could do in helping his preparations for the Test. He has been a great player (who has been on four Lions tours and has won 133 Test caps, leading Ireland to 52 wins in 83 matches) and he is a great bloke, and he showed it here.

He knew that if we won the last Test, he would still be remembered as a Test-winning Lion in 2013, haing started two games out of the three. After all, there were only six players who started all three Tests (Leigh Halfpenny, George North, Jon Davies, Jon Sexton, Adam Jones and Alun-Wyn Jones). The other side of his disappointment was that he had been more fortunate than he had been in New Zealand in 2005, when his tour had been cruelly cut short after only 90 seconds of the first Test when he dislocated his shoulder after a horrible spear tackle from Tana Umaga and Keven Mealamu. He still had a part to play, even if he wasn't actually going to be taking the field in that final Test.

I remember talking to Andy Irvine and Sir Ian McGeechan and they said that the ultimate Lions tourist they had ever encountered or heard of had been the former England prop, Jason Leonard, who had been on three Lions tours to New Zealand in 1993, to South Africa in 1997 and to Australia in 2001, but he had started only two Tests in all that time (both in New Zealand), while coming off the bench in three Tests (once in South Africa and twice in Australia). He had propped on both sides of the scrum in New Zealand and Ian mentioned him in his speech to us when presenting the jerseys before the first Test. He said that Jason had been such a good team man, always helping others.

Given the way Brian conducted himself after being dropped, the way he helped the team prepare and never let his disappointment affect anyone else, it may be that Jason has a rival for the ultimate Lion.

I thought Warren spoke very well about his selection. He had picked a side to beat Australia, not one to keep people happy. 'It's only hard because you are making the decision using your head and not your heart,' he said. 'Then you realise that what comes of making a decision like that is all the peripheral stuff, because it becomes a major story for forty-eight hours and it becomes a debate. I'll go back to the UK after this and say: "Did I make the decision because I believe it's the right decision, or did I make it because it was politically right?"

'I have to put hand on my heart and say it's the right rugby decision. I would hate to think we had made calls to avoid criticism or for reasons of public popularity. Brian is obviously very, very disappointed, as any player would be. It's kind of hard when you've been the number one in your position for so long and first choice on every team you've been a part of.'

I also thought he explained his choice of Alun-Wyn as captain well. 'I don't know why people are trying to make an issue out of that. I don't see it as an issue at all. Alun-Wyn Jones has captained his club side a lot; he has captained Wales in the past. We went and picked what we thought was the best team we think can take the field and do the job. After that it was who do we think can captain the side?'

I thought Alun-Wyn would do a superb job. I have always believed that he would make an excellent captain of Wales, even though he has done the job only once – in the win over Italy in Rome in 2009. In fact, when I was not sure whether I wanted to be captain before the 2011 World Cup, I said to Gats: 'Why don't you pick Alun-Wyn as captain?'

He has always been someone that I have looked up to as a leader, and certainly someone whom I would follow on a rugby field. I have always said about captains that the ones I respect most are not the ones who speak well, or who manage referees well, or who handle press conferences comfortably. I respect the captains who perform well on the field consistently. And Alun-Wyn Jones is a player who always seems to have a good game. Looking at the statistics after a game, he is always high up there in the amount of tackles made, the number of rucks hit or line-outs won.

He is never tired. Or if he is, he will never show that with his body language. Say if we are doing a fitness session, he might be on his last legs but he will still be shouting encouragement at others. 'Come on, only two more circuits to go,' he will scream at the boys. And if he ever makes a mistake in training, he will always drop down and do ten press-ups immediately. He just does that without anyone telling him to do so.

He is obviously a very intelligent bloke, having qualified as a lawyer, but he does make me laugh when he talks to himself, especially at scrummage time. He says things like: 'I can go all day, you Big Red Machine.' That is what he calls himself: The Big Red Machine. I know it took some of the non-Welsh Lions on this tour by surprise at first. The Welsh boys are used to it by now. 'What is Alun-Wyn on about, talking about "The Big Red Machine" when he goes into a scrum?' some of the others asked. I knew he would be a good leader and I made sure I shook his hand as soon as I could after the announcement.

It was during that training session on the day of the team announcement in Noosa when I felt certain we would clinch the series. I said that I thought that would be the case after the Test in Melbourne, but events that day merely confirmed my initial thoughts.

The session itself was not necessarily of the best quality, but there was a certain venom to it. It was edgy and physical, as the training sessions often are after the team has been announced. If it had been too slick and all the players had been out there laughing and giggling, I would have been concerned. But instead there was nervous tension in the air and I knew everyone was in the right place mentally. The slickness could come later in the week.

I was watching that session while sitting on the tackle bags at the side of the field with analyst Rhys Long, and I remember looking at the squad training and saying: 'This is the best team we have picked all tour.' I was really happy with the selection. I made that comment even though I wasn't in the team, but I looked at Sean O'Brien, my replacement, and I saw a world-class player. He was one of the players I had really wanted to play alongside on the tour. I would have loved to have started a match with him, but the only time I did spend on the field with him was when he came on in the second Test for Jamie Heaslip for a short period before I was injured. Sean had been playing really well, and he is a big physical specimen. For the game plan we were going to implement in that third Test, I remember thinking it was definitely the best side we could have picked.

Australia had sprung a surprise in their team selection, too, by recalling George Smith at openside flanker. Smith was nearly 33 and his last Test had been against Wales in Cardiff in 2009 when we had both been wearing No. 19 shirts as we came off the bench in Australia's 33-12 win. Smith had spent the last four seasons playing club rugby in Japan, after a spell at Toulon, and he had returned to Australia only because the Brumbies had been stretched by injuries and needed short-term cover. A knee injury had ruled him out of contention for the first two Tests against us. He had played in all three Tests against the Lions in 2001 and would become only the fourth Australian to play against the Lions on two separate tours – the other three had only done so as far back as the 1959 and 1967 tours.

Smith was the only change to the Australian side that had won 16-15 in Melbourne, and he replaced Michael Hooper, who dropped to the bench instead of Liam Gill. Australia did make one other change on the bench, where back-row forward Ben McCalman came in for centre Rob Horne, as they opted for a six-to-two split between forwards and backs, with only Nick Phipps and Jesse Mogg covering all the backline positions.

Looking at the two line-ups, I felt Australia might find it difficult to cope with the power of the team that Warren had chosen. For that's what he had done. At every point he had gone for power. Jamie Roberts was always going to play if fit. He is so influential in Warren's game plan, because he is so good at getting over the gain line, and, amid the uproar about

Brian, it was probably forgotten how well Jon Davies had played at outside centre against the New South Wales Waratahs the Saturday before the first Test. Also our kicking game had not always been as good as we would have liked in the Melbourne Test, so Jon's left boot could be useful in that respect. That Manu Tuilagi was on the bench was just a continuation of Warren's power theme.

By kick-off, I was as pumped up for the game as if I was playing. When you are in the dungeon of a changing room, you do not see the build-up of the fans and the noise and you have to keep a cool head. But here in Sydney I was out there, taking pictures on my phone, taking it all in and, as the game unfolded, I was jumping up and down so much I had to be careful not to injure my hamstring again. I completely forgot about it in the moment.

And I did plenty of jumping up and down as we won 41-16. Yes, 41-16! Warren's selection was proved to be totally right, as we completely dominated Australia physically. Our scrummage destroyed theirs and at every breakdown and contact we seemed to be stronger and more powerful. It was wonderful to watch, as in the 125th anniversary of the Lions when we won a Test series for the first time since Martin Johnson's team won in South Africa in 1997. Sixteen long years came to an end in front of a huge crowd of 83,702 in the ANZ Stadium. It was Australia's heaviest defeat against the Lions since fixtures began in 1899, with the 41 points scored being ten more than the previous highest against Australia in 1966.

We scored four tries through Alex Corbisiero, George North, Jon Sexton and Jamie Roberts. Leigh Halfpenny kicked 21 points, with five penalties and three conversions, as well as helping create two of those four tries. Those 21 points from Leigh were an individual record for a Lions Test, overtaking the 20 scored by both Jonny Wilkinson (against Argentina in the one-off Test in Cardiff in 2005) and Stephen Jones (in the second Test against South Africa in 2009). It meant that he ended the tour having kicked 40 from 45 attempts. His 49 points for the Test series were another record, beating the 41 scored by Neil Jenkins in South Africa in 1997. It was little surprise that he was named man of the match, and then man of the series. If you also remember that he had been man of the Six Nations Championship too, then it had been some year for Leigh.

For me the highlight of the celebrations that followed that night was seeing Leigh, the most professional guy in the squad, finally let his guard down and enjoy himself with the boys. He normally puts himself under so much pressure and is so demanding of himself. So he thoroughly deserved all those awards and the chance to celebrate afterwards, especially when you consider how down he was after the second Test in Melbourne.

You just suspected it was going to be our night from the very start. Alun-Wyn Jones won the toss and elected to kick off, and Jon Sexton's kick was immediately dropped by Will Genia. It was an uncharacteristic mistake from such a great player, but it handed us an initiative we were not going to let slip. From that first scrummage of the game, we won a free kick, as it became immediately obvious that, with Corbisiero back after his calf problem and on fire, we were going to be on top in that area of the game. It helped that the referee was Romain Poite, who always tends to reward the dominant scrummage in a match. In the rest of the game, we won another free kick and five penalties at the scrummage and Australia also lost prop Ben Alexander to the sin bin for collapsing. He didn't return to the field after that. It was a great night for our forwards coach, Graham Rowntree. All his hard work paid off here.

From that first free kick we ran the ball, and three phases later Corbs was evading Benn Robinson's tackle to score. Mike Phillips had tapped to send Tommy Bowe towards the line. He was stopped five metres short, but Sean O'Brien and Alun-Wyn carried it on, before Phillsy took the ball from a ruck under the Australian posts to feed Corbs on his left. The game was only 77 seconds old and, with Leigh kicking the conversion, we were 7-0 up.

That was followed by a Pence penalty won by Dan Lydiate after a tackle on Joe Tamone. Christian Lealiifano kicked a penalty in response, but then three scrummages brought another nine points in 13 minutes for us and Leigh, the last of them after Alexander had been given his yellow card, and when his ten-minute period was over, he was replaced by Sekope Kepu. We were 19-3 up.

Australia had also lost George Smith to the concussion bin after a horrible clash of heads with Richard Hibbard in the fifth minute. It was a brutal collision and was replayed on TV over and over again afterwards. But Richard is a real no-nonsense, tough character from Taibach near Port Talbot, and I'll remember to avoid any clashes like that with his granite-like head when we next play the Ospreys!

Smith returned, but Israel Folau didn't, after pulling a hamstring on 25 minutes. Folau's replacement was Jesse Mogg, who looked dangerous and made one stunning break that was only stopped by a brilliant tap tackle from the superb Geoff Parling. That's the thing with Australian teams, though: they never give up a game easily. It looked as if the match had been won, but the Aussies were having none of that just yet. They pressed hard, and from a five-metre scrummage James O'Connor broke through to score. Lealiifano converted, so that it was only 19-10 at half time.

When Lealiifano then kicked two penalties inside six minutes at the start of the second half, Australia had suddenly scored 13 unanswered points and at 19-16, it was very much game on. But I felt it was our destiny to win. When Australia came back, it didn't surprise me, as I thought the start we had had was just too good to be true. I could sense the Lions fans were anxious, but they still made an incredible amount of noise. They played a huge part on the tour as a whole. Indeed, one of my fondest memories of the tour will be the fans in general. Knowing that four countries were all cheering for us and seeing their passion was something very special. I had heard about the role the fans play before the tour and how special they make it, and that was certainly the case in

Australia. They did not disappoint for certain. I would always make time for the fans, whether in the hotel or on the street, as we all appreciated how much money and effort was spent on getting to the other side of the world to support us.

Even with the fans roaring us on, we still needed some superb work to keep them out, even after Leigh had added another penalty to make it 22-16. First, when Kurtley Beale chipped over our defence and picked up, it was Leigh who tackled him in our 22 and prevented an off-load. And then Toby Faletau made a steal that gets more important the more you think about it.

I thought Toby had a massive game. He was immense on the gain line. Mind you, so many people had big games, especially among the forwards, that they will always remember this match. Sean O'Brien tackled himself to a standstill, as did Dan Lydiate. Alun-Wyn had a huge impact, smashing into contact and often off-loading deftly too. And the front row were outstanding, with Hibbard's bravery to the fore (he got up immediately from that collision with Smith) and Adam Jones a rock as always at tight-head prop. As for Corbs, afterwards Warren Gatland said that he was his man of the match, and you could easily see why – the Lions had dominated the scrummage, he had scored that early try, and he seemed to be everywhere.

From Toby's crucial turnover, we counter-attacked and Jon Sexton's kick ahead was taken by George North, who found Jon Davies. He might have been tackled into touch, but we had a territorial position from which we could pounce. When we eventually won the ball again, Jon Sexton brought in Tommy Bowe, who found Jon Davies about 30 metres out. He beat one tackle and found Leigh who surged into the Australian 22 before finding Sexto inside to score. Leigh converted once the television match official had checked on a forward pass, and it was 29-19.

Seven minutes later came the try that finally killed off the Australians. It was begun by Leigh as he gathered a kick on our ten-metre line and counter-attacked, beating two defenders, breaking Genia's tackle and outpacing Tomane, before putting George North clear. Leigh missed his first kick of the evening in attempting the conversion, but now it was 34-19, with little more than ten minutes remaining.

There was more. Seven minutes later, Toby won a line-out and Conor Murray, on for Mike Phillips, fed Jamie Roberts, who came hammering through on a superb angle for our fourth try. Pence converted, and we even tried a 13-man line-out towards the end as we attempted to rub in our physical superiority. But despite our big lead, it was only when there was just five minutes left that I felt it was safe to start to celebrate. I worked out at that stage they needed to score a try every 75 seconds – and I would like to think that I could have backed our defence in that situation!

The boys started to do a bit of a dance on the sidelines. As I've mentioned, Simon Zebo is a good dancer and he had become a bit of a cult figure with the supporters. So when the music came on after a try or conversion, he would do a little dance. At least he wasn't doing them while on the wing this time!

The scenes on the field at the end were incredible. There was so much emotion, passion and delight. There were smiles and tears, as we all hugged each other. And there were some great photographs taken that will, I'm sure, be treasured by everyone for the rest of their lives. But there is one in particular that I have been asked about a few times, and I will try to explain here what it meant. It was one of George North and me where George is obviously making a joke and counting something with his fingers.

The first thing I will say before relating this story is that, as I pointed out when he was accused of being so when pointing a finger at Will Genia while scoring in Brisbane, George is not arrogant, and neither am I. But we both do like the American sporting culture and the confidence they all have as athletes. It is good to come over as humble – and I hope both George and I do that – but inside you have got to have real confidence. I think that I am better than my opposite number every time I go onto a rugby field. I have to think that way. It's like the personal identity statement I settled upon when I first started working with Andy McCann: 'I am the world's best seven.' George is very similar; he backs himself. He knows that he is a good athlete and he knows that he is a good player. Yes, there is a fine line between confidence and arrogance, but you have got to have that confidence.

Anyway, George and I quite enjoy watching the TV programme *Hard Knocks*, which is a reality documentary following a National Football League (NFL) team each season. And in that programme there are players who are arrogant. They are often on the phone to their agents saying things like: 'I'm not getting out of bed for less than five million dollars.' They will then go on to say just how much they are worth. So, after a good match George and I will often indulge in some trash talk. I will say to him in an American accent: 'Boy, you are worth five million dollars!' and that's what we were doing in that photo. It was just mickey-taking out of the NFL players, nothing more.

There was a presentation ceremony at which Alun-Wyn Jones and I were presented with the Tom Richards Trophy. I had decided earlier that I was going to tell Alun-Wyn to come up with me, but, before I could, Andy Irvine said: 'You and Alun-Wyn are going to go up and collect the trophy.'

I replied: 'That's brilliant because I was going to ask him to do that anyway.'

When I told Alun-Wyn what was going to happen, he said: 'No, no, mate. You go up and get it. You are tour captain.'

I told him: 'No way. I'm not going up there unless you do. And anyway, Andy Irvine has said it has been arranged that we should go up together.'

That was typical of Alun-Wyn, showing what a great bloke he is, but there was no way that I could accept his offer. I also wanted Brian O'Driscoll and Paul O'Connell to be recognised, too. I know there had been other captains on tour, such as Dan Lydiate and Rory Best, but I really thought that Brian and Paul should be picked out for their leadership on tour. So I said to them: 'When Alun-Wyn and I collect the trophy, can you two make sure you are behind us, please?'

But unfortunately it was only Alun-Wyn and I who went

up. That was why, when we were photographed later as a cel-ebrating squad behind a big sponsorship board, there was a photograph of Brian and Paul lifting the trophy together. Jon Sexton made sure that happened, and it was a very fitting thing to happen.

So Alun-Wyn and I collected the trophy and then I had to make a speech up there, which is never easy because you do not want to come over as too triumphant. And it also was not easy because I had no idea beforehand that I was going to have to do it. I'd had no prior notice! James Horwill had spoken and I asked Andy Irvine: 'Do I need to say something here?'

'Yeah, just say a few words,' he replied. So I had about five seconds in which to think what to say.

I had to be very aware that there were some extremely despondent Australian players out there, and I did not want to rub it in in any way. So this is what I said, completely off the cuff: 'Firstly, thanks to the Australian boys. It's been an absolutely immense Test series. You made it incredibly tough for us, and you were so unlucky. To our boys a massive, massive well done. We've worked so hard for this. To all the fans who paid thousands and thousands of pounds to travel halfway across the world to watch us play, a huge thank you. It's made our tour. It's been a squad effort – that's over forty players and with the management eighty in total. A huge thank you to everybody and have a good night.'

I was so pleased for Warren Gatland. He had made some big calls and had copped some ridiculous flak. You could tell that it had really affected him. He did, though, retain his sense of humour. Not long after the team announcement, he walked over to a group of the players in the team room and said something like: 'Any chance of winning this weekend please, boys, because I am getting some monumental stick for my selection!' He laughed and walked away, and a couple of boys replied: 'Yeah, don't worry, we will win.' And the team did.

You could see the relief on Gats' face afterwards. He had had the last laugh. He had proved what a great coach he is. He had proved that he knew more than all those critics about team selection. He had got that spot on. He had proved everyone else wrong. He had also proved what a great leader he is. He has always said as Wales coach that he will take the flak so that the players don't have to take it, and this was the definitive example of that. When it could have been the players copping it for losing the second Test in Melbourne, instead it was Gats who was copping it for his selection. But, as he said afterwards: 'The last three or four days have been very, very hard. I had to make a tough decision on Thursday in leaving Brian out. You always doubt decisions, but you have to make those hard calls sometimes.

'We said: "Look, there's going to be a significant amount of fall-out for that and are we prepared to take the flak?" I've taken quite a bit of flak and I don't want to gloat or feel vindicated. It was about the boys today. It was an outstanding performance. We started well, came under some pressure and bounced back again. I said all along that Australia were desperate last week and they brought all their emotion. We felt there was another step up we could bring and we showed that tonight. We scored some fantastic tries – the four tries tonight. I thought Alex Corbisiero was man of the match and the guys deserve a lot of credit.'

The changing room afterwards was the best I have ever experienced. Daniel Craig came in to join us and, to be fair, he did not want to make it about himself. He was quite quiet, but obviously all the boys wanted their photographs taken with him (except for shy old me, as I have said) – they were like kids in a sweet shop. It was strange because out on the field everyone, including Daniel Craig, had been watching the Lions. Now in the changing rooms, it was all the Lions looking starstruck at Daniel Craig.

We had loads of bottles of champagne and it was being sprayed everywhere. The boys were singing, jumping up and down. I have been in changing rooms when Wales have won the Grand Slam or the Six Nations, but this was different. It felt even more special being with boys from four different nations, who only a few months ago were trying to knock each other's heads off, yet here we were celebrating like best mates. I guess that is the magic of the Lions. It was an incredibly special moment.

At one stage, Jon Sexton got hold of a Welsh flag that Leigh Halfpenny had borrowed from his mates in Gorseinon. On it was written the following little poem:

'Leigh Halfpenny is a rock

He loves a high ball and has got a massive ..'

Of course, everyone expects something rude at the end of

that, but it actually says kick! So Sexto and a few other non-Welsh boys suddenly got behind the Welsh flag and started chanting: 'Wales! Wales!' Then the whole changing room joined in and everyone in there was chanting: 'Wales! Wales!' As he jokingly said afterwards: 'A very proud day for me . . . an unbelievable memory winning my first Welsh cap. One I'll remember forever!'

No one got changed for at least an hour and a half after the final whistle, because we were soaking up the atmosphere. After the big celebration, I sat down with a group of the Welsh boys – George North, Jamie Roberts, Alex Cuthbert, Leigh Halfpenny and Jon Davies – to share a (for me) rare beer, but that was all there was in the dressing room apart from champagne. We touched bottles and toasted each other, knowing that we had done it. That was when it started to really sink it. We had all come through the academy system and been through quite a lot together.

After that, Dan Lydiate got changed quite quickly and he, Paul O'Connell and I had a chat in a quiet corner, reflecting on the tour as a whole. Paul was really good to me. I think he saw that I was a little quiet and he emphasised that I had played two Tests and was a series winner. 'You're twenty-four and you've done it, bud,' he said. 'You're a Lions Test-series-winning captain.'

I haven't said this before, but the truth is I was devastated I didn't play in that last game. There is even a part of me that feels like I can't take credit for being the captain of the series victory. When people tell me I'm a Lions series-winning captain, I immediately think: 'Yeah, but I didn't play in the last game.'

I know that I've achieved a lot already in the game at such a young age, but I also recognise that of the four big moments in my career so far, three have not gone as I would have liked. That still rankles and will spur me on. There was the World Cup semi-final in 2011, when I was obviously sent off which then meant missing the third-place play-off against Australia, then the Grand Slam match against France in 2012 in which I had to go off injured at half time, and now this. The Six Nations decider against England was the exception. None of this is meant to be looking for sympathy, as I'm very proud of my career to date, but I think that it is actually a good reality check for me as I go forward.

It was certainly a long celebration in the changing rooms. The only downside of it was that I didn't see my parents during that time. In fact, I didn't get to see them until the following afternoon. I did some press in the morning and then saw them for about four hours in the afternoon. I know they were a little disappointed not to see me after the game, as were the other players' parents. At the Millennium Stadium in Cardiff, there is a brilliant arrangement because the family room is next to the changing rooms, so the players can pop in and out and have the best of both worlds, but that was not the case here.

After leaving the ground, we went to the Sydney Opera House for the official function, but we didn't get there until 1am. And then we went on to a nightclub called Ivy afterwards.

It actually wasn't as wild as I thought it might have been. We had five security guys with us throughout the tour – two of them were former SBS members and the other three were former Marines – and if they ever saw any of the boys' behaviour getting out of hand, they either told them to calm down or just bundled them into a Land Rover and took them back to the hotel. None of us ever argued with them – it wouldn't have been much of a contest!

The Ivy had a pool, so most of the boys ended up jumping in there. I didn't go in because I was worried about my hamstring, but at least I didn't do what Toby Faletau did, and that was throw in a whole heap of clothes and shoes that been left pool-side. I'm not sure anyone really noticed.

I rarely eat McDonald's, but I treated myself to one that night. It was the first one I had had in six months and was bought for me by a fan who refused to let me pay. I had a Big Mac, a cheeseburger and chips and it did not even touch the sides. If there was one night I deserved a treat it was this one.

I am not a big drinker, but I did have a few vodka and cranberry juices after those initial beers. I only drink about twice a year, normally after a Six Nations campaign. I choose not to drink because I know it is not the best thing for me, but I also genuinely do not like the taste or smell of beer. Vodka and cranberry is about the only thing I can drink, and I think that is only because I know there are probably some anti-oxidants in the juice.

I eventually got to bed at about 3am and when I got up at 9am my first sight was of Leigh Halfpenny and Mike Phillips still dressed in the Australian jerseys they had swapped with their opposite numbers. They were stinking! But they were like a double act that day, Pence and Phillsy, as they carried on celebrating without going to bed. As I've said before, it was especially great to see Leigh letting his hair down. He so deserved it.

He had to do a photo shoot that morning, though he was not really in any sort of state. It was lucky he did not have to do press for sure, because he would not have been able to speak, but I think he got away with the photo. He went back to his room, had a shower, and was just about presentable enough.

There was a bus at about 1pm that took the boys down to Bondi Beach for the day. I didn't go, as I was seeing my parents, but Dan Lydiate, who had been with his fiancée Nia all afternoon, and I went down to the beach at about 6pm to join the other boys. I was drinking again! As I said, I don't usually do more than two nights in a year, let alone two nights on the trot, but this was different, I suppose. There was a third night too, on the Monday, before we flew home on the Tuesday, and I was preparing myself to drink again, even if I did not really want to. I was worried that I might get ill because I am so unused to doing anything like this.

Fortunately, Dan Lydiate came back to the room and said that he didn't want to go out either, so we stayed in and ordered room service. I had pizza and he had burger and chips. We put the plates in between the beds and tucked our napkins into our shirts and had a romantic dinner for two!

That Sunday was the day when Stuart Hogg was seen coming out of the hotel wearing just his very skimpy swimming trunks. He had a set of them – in Scottish, Irish, Welsh, English and Lions colours with emblems – but he had not been able to wear them in public during the official part of the tour because they were not supplied by one of the Lions' sponsors. Now he was free to do what he wanted, and he duly sported the red Lions pair. He's a great laugh is Hoggy, and he definitely showed it that day.

There was one last formal part of the tour before our flight home on the Tuesday, when we had to undergo a thorough medical for insurance purposes so the clubs were happy when we got back. My brother Ben had just started as a physio at the Cardiff Blues, having moved on from the Newport Gwent Dragons, so it was great to have him working on my hamstring when I got home. I even went on holiday down to Pembrokeshire in west Wales with him and his girlfriend, Rhian, so that he could treat me there, too. We were also joined by my parents, Rachel, my sister Holly, her husband Chris and their son Harrison. While we were there, my dad pulled a hamstring playing tennis with Ben, and Chris hurt his shoulder too, so poor old Ben was busy, even if he was supposed to be on holiday.

Just before we went away, however, I had been to London for a scan on my hamstring and John Miles, the Cardiff Blues' medical chief, then commented on it in a statement, saying: 'Sam suffered a grade three tear to his left hamstring in the second Lions Test against Australia on 29 June. He has had a scan with specialists in London yesterday which has shown the injury is already healing. He therefore does not need surgery, but will require a period of rehabilitation between twelve to sixteen weeks from the date of the injury. His re-habilitation will focus on a range of motion, flexibility and specific strengthening of the hamstring in order for him to return to full health.'

But despite this very long lay-off, nothing could spoil what we had achieved in Australia. The previous eight weeks had been the best rugby experience of my life and winning the series against Australia is by far the biggest achievement of my career. It only makes me realise how much I would love to cap-tain the British and Irish Lions again for the tour of New Zealand in 2017, if I was ever fortunate enough to get the chance.

I remember talking to Tommy Bowe early on in the tour when I was rooming with him, and we were discussing players who had been unlucky to have missed out on selection because of injury. He said that Stephen Ferris had found it tough, because having been in South Africa four years ago had made it worse to be unavailable for this tour. I did not really appre-ciate that at the time, because our chat was early on, but having experienced eight weeks with this group of players, I know exactly that feeling and understand how much he must have regretted missing this tour. I know I want to have this experience again, especially as I think the Lions should have a great chance of beating New Zealand.

Looking back on it now, I know that to captain the Lions to

a series win was beyond my childhood dreams, even if my hamstring injury prevented me from playing in that decisive third Test. Although there was so much focus on me in that role, I have to say that the Lions captaincy is the easiest I've ever had. I actually loved it. Forget all that reluctance about wanting to be captain of Wales. It makes me want to be Wales captain now.

As I said to the press after the series victory: 'As soon as I saw the squad for this tour, I thought we were going to win. Going into this Lions tour, the fact we had lost the last three wouldn't have bothered me at all. It doesn't even enter my thought process. Whoever is going to be involved in four years' time, for some players it might have given them more optimism but for me, I don't need to win a match to prove to myself I can do something. I'll always believe it from day one anyway. Anyone who says the Lions have no chance of beating New Zealand is talking rubbish.'

It had struck me during a training session in Noosa on the Wednesday before the final Test in Sydney what the group could be capable of. One of the computers at the side of the pitch that was receiving live GPS data was showing that the current age of the players taking part in that session was 25. I thought to myself that if that same group of players is still available in four years' time, they will be hitting their straps as 29-year-olds. Just imagine how good they could be. A lot can happen between now and then, of course, but there is a young group of players here who potentially have the opportunity to come back together again and try to win a Test series against the All Blacks. It is an exciting prospect.

The flight home was obviously long, so there was time for some more photos with the trophy. I am afraid that I will have to disappoint a few people here, and confess that the photo taken of me asleep with the trophy in my arms was not genuine. I just did that for a second or two for a laugh and the snap was taken. When people were later tweeting me saying, 'That's how much it means to you,' I was thinking: 'Have you tried sleeping with that thing? It would be so uncomfortable!'

Before we had taken off, though, Alun-Wyn and I had gone into the plane's cockpit and had our photos taken with captains' hats on. That was a good experience, and a good photo, too. When we arrived back home at Heathrow Airport on Wednesday 10 July, there were more than a hundred fans there to welcome us, and there was a big cheer when I appeared, with the Tom Richards Trophy on top of my baggage.

It was time for some last photos and one last interview, even though I was feeling absolutely knackered. I can never sleep on planes, and here I was sweating, as I had to push this pretty heavy trophy on my baggage. I was happy – of course I was – but I was also dog-tired. I had no idea what time it was. One of the photographers said: 'Come on, Sam, smile!' I felt a bit bad about that but I really had no energy left.

It was weird as we all went our separate ways, and tried to say goodbye to everyone. That was impossible, but there were some emotional hugs and cheerios. It was like watching a really good television series, and then suddenly it's over, and you don't know what to do. All the Irish boys turned right to catch a connecting flight, while the rest of us walked straight on. We got our bags and then the English and Scottish boys gradually separated, so that it was only the Welsh boys left waiting for our bus back to Wales.

We got on and it was as if we were back in a Wales camp straight away. As we crossed the Severn Bridge, the driver put on Tom Jones's 'Green, Green Grass of Home'. We all felt so relaxed. The sun was out and we knew that we were about to have four weeks of holiday. When we arrived back at the Vale Resort, there was a children's choir there waiting for us, and they sang beautifully. I made sure that I thanked the teacher with them and they had some photos taken with us. My brother Ben was there to pick me up, and that was that. My 2013 Lions adventure was over. But it had been some adventure.

'It is a lot cleaner than it was Saturday night, that's for sure,' I had said about the trophy in that final tour interview. 'There were a few bottles of champagne in the trophy. It is a great feeling. It has been a long time coming, this Lions tour, so it is nice to come back with a trophy. It has only been done nine times in one hundred and twenty-five years, so all the players know they are part of a very prestigious group and are very proud of that.

'It won't sink in for a long time, I think. It feels quite surreal being part of a Lions touring party. Only four years ago, I got capped for Wales during a Lions tour. I got on the development tour and I never thought I would be in this situation four years later. Maybe in a few months' time or a few years' time I might watch back a DVD and realise what we achieved.'

What we had achieved was a series victory, the first in 16 years. That's what we went to Australia for, and that's what we returned with.

Having had some time to think about it now, it still feels surreal and it still hasn't sunk in. I have been talking to Leigh Halfpenny about it, and we both agreed that we don't think we will fully realise what we have done until after our careers have finished.

When we got back, I wanted a media and appearance blackout for the five weeks I had off after the tour, so I could escape from the pressures of rugby and spend some quality time with Rachel, my family and my friends. And I got that, and thoroughly enjoyed it. I made only two public appearances. The first came a week after I landed when I went back to my old primary school, Llanishen Fach in Rhiwbina, and to my old high school, Whitchurch.

When I went to Whitchurch, I was there for about six hours signing autographs and doing photographs. I also did a question-and-answer session in the hall in front of 300 pupils and teachers. The applause I got going into the room was amazing. It's a great feeling and very humbling to find out how proud you have made people feel. I owe a lot to Whitchurch. They were great in allowing me to pursue rugby as a highly dedicated young boy, and in using the gym whenever I wanted. I also had wonderful technical help from the teachers, in particular Steve Williams and Gwyn Morris, whom I have already mentioned here. I still stay in contact with both them today.

When Gwyn found out that we don't actually get a cap for representing the Lions, he searched high and low to find one and got it embroidered with 'Lions winning captain 2013 Sam Warburton'. The school presented this to me after the Q & A, and I felt extremely emotional at this point. It felt like only yesterday that I was sitting in the same grounds, classrooms and yards dreaming about playing for the Lions. In what seems like the blink of an eye, I am in the privileged position I am today.

It proves to me that a decade of sacrifice, turning down nights out, not drinking beers, not eating chocolate at Christmas, training every day of every school holiday I had, and pounding the gyms and streets of north Cardiff, and running late at night for all my school years was worth every single minute. My granddad Keith, who passed away after the 2011 Rugby World Cup, had always told me: 'What you put in in life, is what you get out.' I have always believed that, and it's an important message to share: you will get your rewards if you work hard enough.

I can go home now and sit on my favourite single seat in my lounge, with my Lions Test jersey framed above me on the wall. The huge satisfaction and honour I feel that I achieved in wearing that jersey is something nobody can ever take away from me.

Nothing more needs to be said, except maybe one of my favourite phrases: Happy Days!

Lions Tour Statistics

Saturday 1 June, v Barbarians, Hong Kong Stadium, Attendance: 28,643

LIONS 59
Tries: O'Connell, Phillips (2), Davies, Cuthbert (2), Lydiate, A-W.Jones
Penalties: Farrell (3)
Conversions: Farrell (3), Sexton (2)

BARBARIANS 8
Try: Fotuali'I
Penalty: Daly

Stuart Hogg	15	Jared Payne	
Alex Cuthbert	14	Joe Rokocoko	
Jonathan Davies	13	Elliot Daly	
Jamie Roberts	12	Casey Laulala	
Sean Maitland	11	Takudzwa Ngwneya	
Owen Farrell	10	Nick Evans	
Mike Phillips	9	Dimitri Yachvili	
Mako Vunipola	1	Paul James	
Richard Hibbard	2	Schalk Brits	
Adam Jones	3	Martin Castrogiovanni	
Richie Gray	4	Marco Wentzel	
Paul O'Connell (c)	5	Dean Mumm	
Dan Lydiate	6	Samu Manoa	
Justin Tipuric	7	Sam Jones	
Toby Faletau	8	Sergio Parisse	

Replacements:

Tom Youngs	16	Leonardo Ghiraldini	
Cian Healy	17	Duncan Jones	
Matt Stevens	18	Andrea Lo Cicero	
Alun-Wyn Jones	19	James Hamilton	
Jamie Heaslip	20	Imanol Harinordoquy	
Conor Murray	21	Kahn Fotuali'I	
Jonathan Sexton	22	James Hook	
George North	23	Mike Tindall	

Referee: Steve Walsh

Lions Triumphant

Wednesday 5 June, v Western Force, Patersons Stadium, Attendance: 35,103

LIONS 69

Tries: Sexton, O'Driscoll (2), Croft, Farrell, Heaslip, Vunipola, Bowe, Parling
Penalties: Halfpenny (2)
Conversions: Halfpenny (9)

WESTERN FORCE 17

Tries: Brown, McCaffrey
Penalty: Sheehan
Conversions: Sheehan (2)

Lions		Western Force
Leigh Halfpenny	15	Sam Christie
Tommy Bowe	14	Dane Haylett-Petty
Brian O'Driscoll (c)	13	Ed Stubbs
Manu Tuilagi	12	Chris Tuatara-Morrison
George North	11	Corey Brown
Jonathan Sexton	10	Sam Norton-Knight
Conor Murray	9	Brett Sheehan
Cian Healy	1	Salesi Manu
Rory Best	2	James Hilterbrand
Dan Cole	3	Salesi Ma'afu
Alun-Wyn Jones	4	Toby Lynn
Ian Evans	5	Phoenix Battye
Tom Croft	6	Angus Cottrell
Sean O'Brien	7	Matt Hodgson
Jamie Heaslip	8	Richard Brown

Replacements:

Tom Youngs	16	Hugo Roach
Mako Vunipola	17	Sione Kolo
Matt Stevens	18	Tim Metcher
Geoff Parling	19	Ben Matwijow
Toby Faletau	20	Locky McCaffrey
Ben Youngs	21	Alby Mathewson
Owen Farrell	22	Nick Haining
Sean Maitland	23	Solomoni Rasolea

Referee: Glen Jackson

Saturday 8 June, v Queensland Reds, Suncorp Stadium, Attendance: 50,136

LIONS 22
Try: B.Youngs
Penalties: Farrell (5)
Conversion: Farrell

QUEENSLAND REDS 12
Tries: Morahan, Frisby
Conversion: Cooper

Stuart Hogg	15	Ben Lucas
Alex Cuthbert	14	Rod Davies
Manu Tuilagi	13	Ben Tapuai
Jonathan Davies	12	Anthony Faingaa
Tommy Bowe	11	Luke Morahan
Owen Farrell	10	Quade Cooper
Ben Youngs	9	Nick Frisby
Mako Vunipola	1	Ben Daley
Tom Youngs	2	James Hanson
Matt Stevens	3	Greg Holmes
Richie Gray	4	Ed O'Donoghue
Geoff Parling	5	Adam Wallace-Harrison
Dan Lydiate	6	Ed Quirk
Sam Warburton (c)	7	Beau Robinson
Toby Faletau	8	Jake Schatz

Replacements:

Richard Hibbard	16	Albert Anae
Dan Cole	17	Sam Denny
Adam Jones	18	Jono Owen
Paul O'Connell	19	Radike Samo
Justin Tipuric	20	Jarrad Butler
Conor Murray	21	Jonathon Lance
Jonathan Sexton	22	Mike Harris
George North	23	Dominic Shipperley

Referee: Jaco Peyper

Lions Triumphant

Tuesday 11 June, v Combined NSW/Queensland Country, Hunter Stadium, Attendance: 20,071

LIONS 64

Tries: Cuthbert, North (2), Murray, Hogg, Hibbard, O'Driscoll, Halfpenny, O'Brien, Davies
Conversions: Hogg (4), Halfpenny (3)

COMBINED COUNTRY 0

Sean Maitland	15	Nathan Trist
Alex Cuthbert	14	Alex Gibbon
Brian O'Driscoll (c)	13	Lewie Catt
Jamie Roberts	12	Tereta-Junior Siakisini
George North	11	Tom Cox
Stuart Hogg	10	Angus Roberts
Conor Murray	9	Mick Snowden
Alex Corbisiero	1	Haydn Hirsimaki
Richard Hibbard	2	Josh Mann-Rea
Dan Cole	3	Tim Metcher
Richie Gray	4	Phoenix Battye
Ian Evans	5	Blake Enever
Sean O'Brien	6	Richard Stanford
Justin Tipuric	7	Jarrad Butler
Jamie Heaslip	8	Tim Davidson

Replacements:

Rory Best	16	Tom Kearney
Ryan Grant	17	Dylan Evans
Matt Stevens	18	Rikki Abraham
Alun-Wyn Jones	19	Rory Arnold
Toby Faletau	20	Trent Dyer
Mike Phillips	21	Adam McCormack
Jonathan Davies	22	Shaun McCarthy
Leigh Halfpenny	23	Dale Ah-Wang

Referee: Steve Walsh

234

Lions Tour Statistics

Saturday 15 June, v NSW Waratahs, Allianz Stadium, Attendance: 40,805

LIONS 47

Tries: Sexton, Halfpenny (2), Croft, Davies
Penalties: Halfpenny (4)
Conversions: Halfpenny (4), Farrell

NSW WARATAHS 17

Tries: Carter (2)
Penalty: McKibbin
Conversions: McKibbin (2)

Lions		Waratahs
Leigh Halfpenny	15	Drew Mitchell
Sean Maitland	14	Cam Crawford
Jonathan Davies	13	Rob Horne
Jamie Roberts	12	Tom Carter
Simon Zebo	11	Peter Betham
Jonathan Sexton	10	Bernard Foley
Mike Phillips	9	Brendan McKibbin
Mako Vunipola	1	Jeremy Tilse
Tom Youngs	2	John Ulugia
Adam Jones	3	Paddy Ryan
Alun-Wyn Jones	4	Will Skelton
Paul O'Connell	5	Oliver Atkins
Tom Croft	6	Jed Holloway
Sam Warburton (c)	7	Patrick McCutcheon
Jamie Heaslip	8	David Dennis

Replacements:

Richard Hibbard	16	Luke Holmes
Alex Corbisiero	17	Richard Aho
Dan Cole	18	Sam Talakai
Geoff Parling	19	Lopeti Timani
Dan Lydiate	20	A.J.Gilbert
Ben Youngs	21	Matt Lucas
Owen Farrell	22	Ben Volavola
Rob Kearney	23	Tom Kingston

Referee: Jaco Peyper

Lions Triumphant

Tuesday 18 June, v Brumbies, Canberra Stadium, Attendance: 21, 625

LIONS 12		BRUMBIES 14
Penalties: Hogg (2), Farrell (2)		*Try*: Kuridrani
		Penalties: Mogg (3)

LIONS		BRUMBIES
Rob Kearney	15	Jesse Mogg
Christian Wade	14	Henry Speight
Brad Barritt	13	Tevita Kuridrani
Billy Twelvetrees	12	Andrew Smith
Shane Williams	11	Clyde Rathbone
Stuart Hogg	10	Matt Toomua
Ben Youngs	9	Ian Prior
Ryan Grant	1	Scott Sio
Rory Best (c)	2	Siliva Siliva
Matt Stevens	3	Ruan Smith
Richie Gray	4	Leon Power
Ian Evans	5	Sam Carter
Sean O'Brien	6	Scott Fardy
Justin Tipuric	7	Colby Faingaa
Toby Faletau	8	Peter Kimlin

Replacements:

Richard Hibbard	16	Josh Mann-Rea
Alex Corbisiero	17	Jean-Pierre Smith
Dan Cole	18	Chris Cocca
Geoff Parling	19	Ettienne Oosthuizen
Dan Lydiate	20	Jordan Smiler
Conor Murray	21	Mark Swanepoel
Owen Farrell	22	Robbie Coleman
Simon Zebo	23	Zack Holmes

Referee: Jerome Garces

Saturday 22 June, First Test v Australia, Suncorp Stadium, Brisbane, Attendance: 52,499

LIONS 23

Tries: North, Cuthbert
Penalties: Halfpenny (3)
Conversions: Halfpenny (2)

AUSTRALIA 21

Tries: Folau (2)
Penalties: O'Connor, Beale (2)
Conversion: O'Connor

Leigh Halfpenny	15	Berrick Barnes
Alex Cuthbert	14	Israel Folau
Brian O'Driscoll	13	Adam Ashley-Cooper
Jonathan Davies	12	Christian Lealiifano
George North	11	Digby Ioane
Jonathan Sexton	10	James O'Connor
Mike Phillips	9	Will Genia
Alex Corbisiero	1	Benn Robinson
Tom Youngs	2	Stephen Moore
Adam Jones	3	Ben Alexander
Alun-Wyn Jones	4	Kane Douglas
Paul O'Connell	5	James Horwill
Tom Croft	6	Ben Mowen
Sam Warburton (c)	7	Michael Hooper
Jamie Heaslip	8	Wycliff Palu

Replacements:

Richard Hibbard	16	Saia Faingaa
Mako Vunipola	17	James Slipper
Dan Cole	18	Sekope Kepu
Geoff Parling	19	Rob Simmons
Dan Lydiate	20	Liam Gill
Ben Youngs	21	Nick Phipps
Owen Farrell	22	Pat McCabe
Sean Maitland	23	Kurtley Beale

Referee: Chris Pollock

Lions Triumphant

Lions		Australia
344	Metres	438
6	Clean breaks	6
16	Defenders beaten	9
108	Passes	127
121	Tackles	125
9	Missed tackles	16
6	Turnovers won	2
12/0	Line-outs won/lost	5/0
5/3	Scrums won/lost	3/0
12	Penalties conceded	7

Lions player stats

Most metres carried	George North 66
	Leigh Halfpenny 32
	Jonathan Sexton 31
	Alex Cuthbert 31
Most tackles made	Sam Warburton 14
	Brian O'Driscoll 11
	Jonathan Davies 10
Most turnovers won	Jamie Heaslip 2

Tuesday 25 June, v Melbourne Rebels, AAMI Park, Attendance: 28,658

LIONS 35

Tries: Murray, Maitland, O'Brien, penalty try, Youngs
Conversions: Farrell (3), Hogg (2)

MELBOURNE REBELS 0

Manu Tuilagi	13	Jason Woodward
Sean Maitland	14	Tom English
Rob Kearney	15	Mitch Inman
Brad Barritt	12	Rory Sidey
Simon Zebo	11	Lachlan Mitchell
Owen Farrell	10	Bryce Hegarty
Conor Murray	9	Luke Burgess
Ryan Grant	1	Nic Henderson
Richard Hibbard	2	Ged Robinson
Dan Cole	3	Laurie Weeks
Richie Gray	4	Hugh Pyle
Ian Evans	5	Cadeyrn Neville
Dan Lydiate (c)	6	Jarrod Saffy
Sean O'Brien	7	Scott Fuglistaller
Toby Faletau	8	Gareth Delve

Replacements:

Rory Best	16	Pat Leafa
Tom Court	17	Paul Alo-Emile
Matt Stevens	18	Cruze Ah-Nau
Tom Croft	19	Luke Jones
Justin Tipuric	20	Jordy Reid
Ben Youngs	21	Nic Stirzaker
Billy Twelvetrees	22	Angus Roberts
Stuart Hogg	23	Cooper Vuna

Referee: Glen Jackson

Saturday 29 June, Second Test v Australia, Etihad Stadium, Melbourne, Attendance: 56,771

LIONS 15
Penalties: Halfpenny (5)

AUSTRALIA 16
Try: Ashley-Cooper
Penalties: Lealiifano (3)
Conversion: Lealiifano

Leigh Halfpenny	15	Kurtley Beale
Tommy Bowe	14	Israel Folau
Brian O'Driscoll	13	Adam Ashley-Cooper
Jonathan Davies	12	Christian Lealiifano
George North	11	Joseph Tomane
Jonathan Sexton	10	James O'Connor
Ben Youngs	9	Will Genia
Mako Vunipola	1	Benn Robinson
Tom Youngs	2	Stephen Moore
Adam Jones	3	Ben Alexander
Alun-Wyn Jones	4	Kane Douglas
Geoff Parling	5	James Horwill
Dan Lydiate	6	Ben Mowen
Sam Warburton (c)	7	Michael Hooper
Jamie Heaslip	8	Wycliff Palu

Replacements:

Richard Hibbard	16	Saia Faingaa
Ryan Grant	17	James Slipper
Dan Cole	18	Sekope Kepu
Tom Croft	19	Rob Simmons
Sean O'Brien	20	Liam Gill
Conor Murray	21	Nick Phipps
Owen Farrell	22	Rob Horne
Alex Cuthbert	23	Jesse Mogg

Referee: Craig Joubert

Lions Tour Statistics

Lions		Australia
140	Metres	459
0	Clean breaks	4
7	Defenders beaten	14
70	Passes	150
140	Tackles	71
14	Missed tackles	7
12	Turnovers won	6
12/1	Line-outs won/lost	10/2
4/3	Scrums won/lost	7/1
11	Penalties conceded	14

Lions player stats

Most metres carried

Jonathan Sexton 40
Leigh Halfpenny 13
Jonathan Davies 12
Jamie Heaslip 12

Most tackles made

Geoff Parling 14
Mako Vunipola 14
Dan Lydiate 13

Most turnovers won

Mako Vunipola 3
Sam Warburton 3

Lions Triumphant

Saturday 6 July, Third Test v Australia, ANZ Stadium, Sydney, Attendance: 83,702

LIONS 41
Tries: Corbisiero, Sexton, North, Roberts
Penalties: Halfpenny (5)
Conversions: Halfpenny (3)

AUSTRALIA 16
Try: O'Connor
Penalties: Lealiifano (3)
Conversion: Lealiifano

Leigh Halfpenny	15	Kurtley Beale
Tommy Bowe	14	Israel Folau
Jonathan Davies	13	Adam Ashley-Cooper
Jamie Roberts	12	Christian Lealiifano
George North	11	Joseph Tomane
Jonathan Sexton	10	James O'Connor
Mike Phillips	9	Will Genia
Alex Corbisiero	1	Benn Robinson
Richard Hibbard	2	Stephen Moore
Adam Jones	3	Ben Alexander
Alun-Wyn Jones (c)	4	Kane Douglas
Geoff Parling	5	James Horwill
Dan Lydiate	6	Ben Mowen
Sean O'Brien	7	George Smith
Toby Faletau	8	Wycliff Palu

Replacements:

Tom Youngs	16	Saia Faingaa
Mako Vunipola	17	James Slipper
Dan Cole	18	Sekope Kepu
Richie Gray	19	Rob Simmons
Justin Tipuric	20	Ben McCalman
Conor Murray	21	Michael Hooper
Owen Farrell	22	Nick Phipps
Manu Tuilagi	23	Jesse Mogg

Referee: Romain Poite

Lions Tour Statistics

Lions		Australia
339	Metres	423
6	Clean breaks	4
19	Defenders beaten	18
94	Passes	126
132	Tackles	121
18	Missed tackles	19
8	Turnovers won	7
10/2	Line-outs won/lost	12/1
10/0	Scrums won/lost	3/3
11	Penalties	9

Lions player stats

Most metres carried

Leigh Halfpenny 88
George North 55
Jamie Roberts 31

Most tackles made

Alun-Wyn Jones 13
Sean O'Brien 13
Jonathan Davies 10
Geoff Parling 10

Most turnovers won

Seven players with one each

Lions Squad for Tour of Australia 2013

Player	Country	Position	Appearances	Points
Brad Barritt	England	Centre	2	0
Rory Best	Ireland	Hooker	2+2	0
Tommy Bowe	Ireland	Wing	4	5 (1T)
Dan Cole	England	Prop	3+6	0
Alex Corbisiero	England	Prop	3+2	5 (1T)
Tom Court	Ireland	Prop	0+1	0
Tom Croft	England	Lock	3+2	10 (2T)
Alex Cuthbert	Wales	Wing	4	20 (4T)
Jonathan Davies	Wales	Centre	6+1	15 (3T)
Ian Evans	Wales	Lock	4	0
Toby Faletau	Wales	Back row	5+2	0
Owen Farrell	England	Fly-half	3+4	51 (1T, 10PG, 8C)
Ryan Grant	Scotland	Prop	2+1	0
Richie Gray	Scotland	Lock	5+1	0
Leigh Halfpenny	Wales	Full-back	5+1	114 (3T, 19PG, 21C)
Cian Healy	Ireland	Prop	1+1	0
Jamie Heaslip	Ireland	No 8	5+1	5 (1T)
Richard Hibbard	Wales	Hooker	4+5	5 (1T)
Stuart Hogg	Scotland	Full-back	4+1	23 (1T, 2PG, 4C)
Gethin Jenkins	Wales	Prop	-	-
Adam Jones	Wales	Prop	5+1	0
Alun-Wyn Jones	Wales	Lock	5+2	5 (1T)
Rob Kearney	Ireland	Full-back	2+1	0
Dan Lydiate	Wales	Back row	5+3	5 (1T)
Sean Maitland	Scotland	Wing	4+1	5 (1T)
Conor Murray	Ireland	Scrum-half	3+4	10 (2T)
George North	Wales	Wing	5+2	20 (4T)
Sean O'Brien	Ireland	Back row	5+1	10 (2T)
Paul O'Connell	Ireland	Lock	3+1	5 (1T)
Brian O'Driscoll	Ireland	Centre	4	15 (3T)

Lions Tour Statistics

Geoff Parling	England	Lock	3+4	5 (1T)
Mike Phillips	Wales	Scrum-half	4+1	10 (2T)
Jamie Roberts	Wales	Centre	4	5 (1T)
Jonathan Sexton	Ireland	Fly-half	5+2	19 (3T, 2C)
Matt Stevens	England	Prop	2+4	0
Justin Tipuric	Wales	Flanker	3+3	0
Manu Tuilagi	England	Centre	3+1	0
Billy Twelvetrees	England	Centre	1+1	0
Mako Vunipola	England	Prop	4+3	5 (1T)
Christian Wade	England	Wing	1	0
Sam Warburton	Wales	Flanker	4	0
Shane Williams	Wales	Wing	1	0
Ben Youngs	England	Scrum-half	3+4	10 (2T)
Tom Youngs	England	Hooker	4+3	0
Simon Zebo	Ireland	Wing	2+1	0

Acknowledgements

I would like to express my gratitude to the many people who helped me through this book.

First, Steve James, who helped me write it and did such a great job of putting my thoughts and experiences down on paper.

Second, my agent Derwyn Jones, who I have now known for six years and has been a fantastic advisor, mentor and friend since we first started working together.

A huge thanks in particular to Warren Gatland and all the management, coaching staff and players at the British and Irish Lions for putting their faith in me as a young captain and being incredibly supportive throughout.

My brother and sister for being my biggest supporters and always making me feel proud to have family as great as they are.

None of this would have been possible without all the effort from my mum and dad over the last 15 years of my playing career since I was a boy. Simply put, none of my success would have been possible without their tremendous support.

Last but not least, my wonderful fiancée and soon-to-be wife Rachel. I could not wish for a better life partner.

Picture Credits

Getty Images: Page 1 (top), 2 (top and centre), 3, 4, 5, 6 (top and bottom), 7, 8, 9, 10, 11, 12, 13 (top and centre), 14, 15, 16 (centre)

Sam Warburton: Page 1 (bottom), 2 (bottom), 6 (centre), 13 (bottom), 16 (top and bottom).